March 18, 2003

3/18/03

The Art of Survival
Recovering Landscape Architecture

The Art of Survival

Recovering Landscape Architecture

Kongjian Yu And Mary Padua (Editors)

Acknowledgements

This book is a collection of articles written by different authors over three years. I am thankful to Mary Padua from Hong Kong University for assistance in putting these articles together and carrying out further editing. Mary, who contributed two of the articles, also regularly helps me with English. Dr. Malt Selugga from Peking University and Turenscape, has also been a great support in editing the book. I am thankful to Susan Jakes from *Time* magazine, professor Antje Stockman from Hanover University, Dr. Birgit Linder from Hong Kong University, Gareth George from *Beijing Today*, Dihua Li and Dr. Xili Han from Peking University, and Wei Pang from Turenscape for allowing me to use their articles. I am extremely grateful to the American Society of Landscape Architects (ASLA), Landscape Australia, *Time* and *Topos*—all have been so generous in granting permission to reprint the articles they had originally published. I also thank Jinlei Lu and his colleagues for their hard work in creating the book's layout in a very short period of time.

My own article, *The Art of Survival—Recovering Landscape Architecture*, was written based on my keynote speeches at the IFLA east region conference held in Sydney in May, 2006, and my speech presented at both the 2006 ASLA annual meeting, and the 43rd IFLA World Congress at Minneapolis. I am thankful to the ASLA, The Australia Institute of Landscape Architects, and The International Federation of Landscape Architects for their invitation and generous support.

The selected projects in this book were all a result of teamwork. I thank my colleagues Dihua Li, Wei Pang, Shihong Lin, and my students Xili Han, Hailong Liu, and Lei Zhang for their extensive involvement in one or more of these projects. Many other staff members from Turenscape, and my students from the Graduate School of Landscape Architecture at Peking University, made contributions to these projects and their names are mentioned with the individual projects in the book. I am always proud of both the research team at Peking University and my design team at Turenscape. Without their hard work and creativity, all the projects would be impossible to complete. The projects selected for inclusion in the book have generally received international awards, and it was these awards that have encouraged us to work hard to face the challenging situation in China.

Kongjian Yu

Dean and Professor, The Graduate School of Landscape Architecture, Peking University and President, Turenscape, Beijing, China

August 1, 2006

Foreword

The Art of Survival: Recovering Landscape Architecture is a remarkable compendium of important concepts. It provides a rich coverage of the major paradigms and trends that influenced the thoughts and practice of landscape architecture in China at the end of the 20th century.

This book is largely the result of the efforts and enthusiasm of the landscape architects of Turenscape and the Graduate School of Landscape Architecture of Peking University, who selected a number of projects, texts, and essays by pioneering landscape architect Kongjian Yu.

Professor Yu describes modern China as having both an identity and an ecological crisis. He is determined to create an appropriately modern and suitably Chinese approach in his writings, in the new landscape architecture program at the Peking University, and in his projects.

Many developing countries, especially China, are facing two major crises: the crisis of cultural identity confronting globalization and modernization, and the crisis of the people–land relationship due to rapid urbanization and industrialization, in which landscape architecture as a profession must play a key role.

The sheer enormity of the scale and speed of social transformation that China is facing has not been encountered in Western social development. China is now at a stage of reshaping the rural and urban landscape. Environmental and recreational consciousness is increasing along with rising levels of income, prosperity, and education.

Urbanization and globalization have positioned landscape architecture to address three major challenges and opportunities in the coming decades, such as finding solutions to both the energy and the environmental crises, regaining cultural identity, and building a spiritual connection to the earth.

The Art of Survival: Recovering Landscape Architecture is a unique contribution of theory and practice. It is both encyclopedic in its coverage of the antecedents of the ideal paradise or Shangri-La, so beautifully expressed in Chinese mythology as the *land of peach blossoms*, and focused on the origins of landscape architecture in China, establishing bridges between the art of survival and land stewardship, along with the challenges and opportunities for landscape architecture for the new era.

The projects illustrated in the chapters 2, 3, and 4 demonstrate an environmental approach, while educating people about green solutions. They show beautiful and attractive places for the people, reflecting a careful recognition and consideration of the landscape and site surroundings, a respect for the natural environment and a consistent way of thinking of the primacy of *The Poetic Vernacular.*

In these projects by Turenscape, new issues for China are evident. These issues concern— besides the biological and dynamic processes of nature— developing approaches to design which track from a particular place, the context of its natural and cultural landscape, and the associated local traditions of the people.

In formulating the designs the writer is creating a new consciousness for the beauty of the Chinese cultural landscape and native, wild, diverse vegetation—a completely new concept for China.

This book makes it possible to follow unequivocally Professor Yu's statement that the challenge for landscape architecture is to recover its role as an art of survival. The leading task is to re-create a new type of land that sustains humanity, returns people's identity, and makes them happy.

This book will be an invaluable tool in translating theory into action, assisting in the global sharing of knowledge, and raising the quality of the professional debate when policies are considered.

On behalf of the International Federation of Landscape Architects I would like to thank and congratulate Professor Yu on the ambitious scope of this book. It is truly exciting that a leading planning intellectual has designed a publication that spans the conceptual thoughts and the real application of this digital age, and globalization in contemporary landscapes.

Martha Cecilia Fajardo

IFLA President

International Federation of Landscape Architects

Bogotá, August 24, 2006

Contents

Published in Australia in 2006 by
The Images Publishing Group Pty Ltd
ABN 89 059 734 431
6 Bastow Place, Mulgrave, Victoria 3170, Australia
Tel: +61 3 9561 5544 Fax: +61 3 9561 4860
books@imagespublishing.com
www.imagespublishing.com

Copyright © The Images Publishing Group Pty Ltd 2006
The Images Publishing Group Reference Number: 706

ISBN 978 1 86470 251 4 – 1 86470 251 6.

Digital production and print by Everbest Printing Co. Ltd.
in Hong Kong/China

CHINA ARCHITECTURE & BUILDING PRESS

The Art of Survival

Recovering Landscape Architecture

Figure 01 There were, and still are, numerous rural Chinese villages that can be described today as Lands of Peach Blossoms. They are the product of thousands of years of trial and error from our agricultural ancestors. They were described by westerners as poetic and picturesque, places where people and spirits are in harmony. (Photo: Yu, K.J.)

1.1 The Art of Survival: Recovering Landscape Architecture

(Keynote Speech delivered at the 2006 ASLA Annual Meeting and 43rd IFLA World Congress, Minneapolis, USA, October 7, 2006. Reprinted (with extensive editing), from Conference Speaker Summaries.)

Kongjian Yu, ASLA

Dean and Professor, The Graduate School of Landscape Architecture, Peking University and President, Turenscape, Beijing, China

Abstract

In a new era of multiple unprecedented challenges imposed by the processes of industrialization and urbanization, landscape architecture is now on the verge of change in the world, and especially in China. It is time for this profession to take the great opportunity to position itself to play the key role in rebuilding a new *Land of Peach Blossoms* for a new society of urbanized, global, and interconnected people. In order to position itself for this sacred role, landscape architecture must define itself in terms of the art of survival, not just as a descendent of gardening. The profession must re-evaluate the vernacular of the land and the people, and lead the way in urban development by planning and designing an infrastructure of both landscape and ecology, through which landscape can be created and preserved as a medium, and as the connecting link between the land, the people, and the spirits.

Introduction

China is now at the stage of reshaping its rural and urban landscape. Urbanization, globalization, and the spread of materialism have provided an opportunity for landscape architecture as a profession to address the following three major challenges and opportunities in the coming decades. First, a solution must be found to address the energy and environmental crises. Second, cultural identity must be regained, and third, the sense of spiritual connection to the earth must be enhanced. The significance of landscape architecture as a profession in dealing with these worldwide challenges is comprehensive in its scope, examining the complexity of natural and biological processes, cultural and historical influences, and spiritual components.

IFLA president Martha Fajardo says that "Landscape architecture is the profession of the future". The future of the profession is positive and it is in a unique position to deal with the landscape as an agent for positive change. This future will only be ours if we are prepared.

To address this challenge, this paper will focus on several issues regarding the direction in which landscape architecture is headed. These questions include an analysis of the current era, the challenges and opportunities that landscape architecture currently faces, a study of the mission of contemporary landscape architecture and its goal, and finally a look at how landscape architecture can take the lead role in addressing the major challenges of the time. It will also examine the strategies and adjustments landscape architecture should take to meet these challenges and compare the strategies that landscape architects can utilize to fulfill this mission.

1 The Land of Peach Blossoms and the Origin of Landscape Architecture as an Art of Survival

In an ancient Chinese story about a *land of peach blossoms*, told by poet Tao Yuanming (365–427 AD), a fisherman traveling along a stream in a boat chances upon a place framed at both sides by blossoming peach trees. In the legend, the place, the source of the stream, was hidden behind a hill. The land had well-cultivated basins, paths, ditches, was surrounded by lush forest-covered hills, and was connected by a single narrow cave. In this isolated utopian landscape, a community lived happily as a family, where the elderly were healthy and the young were lively. The fisherman was welcomed into the peoples' homes and treated with generous hospitality, and was entertained with wine and bountiful food. After the fisherman left the land of peach blossoms and returned to the city, he could never again find this land. This is, in essence, the original story of *Shangri-La*, a mystical, harmonious valley described in 1933 by British novelist James Hilton in *Lost Horizon*.

Since we have experienced such harmonious landscapes, we believe that there were and still are numerous Chinese rural villages that can be described today as lands of peach blossoms. They are the product of thousands of years of the trials

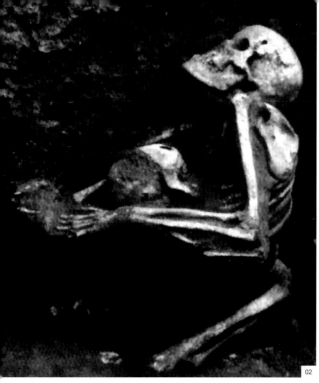

Figure 02 5,000 years ago in the Yellow River Valley, one of the thousands of natural disasters—a flood and a land slide—buried a whole village and its inhabitants. At the very moment when she was being buried in the mud, a young mother protected her baby child, and raised her head, reaching toward the sky, calling on the gods for help. (Photo: Xia, Z.K.)

Figure 03 Da Yu was able to make friends with floods and made wise use of the land to build a city and make fields for crops. Because of his achievement, Da Yu was made the first emperor of feudalist China. The art of survival was the emperor's art of land planning, design and stewardship, and the origin of landscape architecture. (Drawing: unknown)

Figure 04 A Feng Shui master was on hand to select suitable sites for buildings. In any sense Feng Shui was the art of survival and might be described as pre-scientific "landscape architecture". (Drawing: unknown)

and errors of our agricultural ancestors. Natural disasters, including floods, droughts, earthquakes, landslides, soil erosion, as well as the experience of field making, irrigation, and food production, taught our ancestors to create and maintain such lands as the *land of peach blossoms*. It was the skill and art of survival that rendered our landscape productive, safe, beautiful, and meaningful (*Figure 01*).

Four thousand years ago in China's Yellow River Valley, during one of several thousand natural disasters, a village was completely buried by a flood and subsequent landslide, killing all of its inhabitants. When a mother was being buried in the mud, she protected her baby child, raised her head, stretched her arms, and called the gods for help (*Figure 02*). The responding god, Da Yu, was considered a deity who was able to make friends with the floods, and who began to use rules and measures, and made wise use of the land to select a safe place for the people to build a city. Da Yu was China's first emperor (*Figure 03*).

Thus, landscape architecture had its origins in combination with the art of survival and the emperor's leadership.

It was this emperor's art of survival and land stewardship, which evolved over thousands of years of trial and error, that helped the disaster-stricken Chinese people select safe places for their settlements. They tilled fields yet kept the soil safe from erosion, diverted water for irrigation, and selected the right plants for food production (*Figure 04*).

Unfortunately, they did not appreciate the real traditional landscape of the Chinese vernacular of the *land of peach blossoms*, because they belonged to the lower culture that survived because of subsistence—a culture which was long associated with labouring and inferiority.

Figure 05a The "Land of Peach Blossoms" by an artist depicting the Grand View Garden built in the 1600s in China's last feudalist dynasty, the Qin. It was also known as "Garden of a Thousand Gardens". The basic model for each of the individual gardens was "Land of Peach Blossoms", which contained villas, pavilions, streams and bridges, exotic flowers, strangely formed rockery, and was surrounded by manmade hills. What was missing in this phony Land of Peach Blossoms was authentic productive fields and natural processes. (Courtesy Yuan Ming Yuan)

Figure 05b The Grand View Garden, The fake "Land of Peach Blossoms", was the first target burnt down by the invading western armies in 1860. It symbolizes the slow decay of feudalistic China, a period which ended in 1911 when the last emperor was forced to abdicate. (Photo: Yu, K.J.)

Figure 06 The art of foot binding was a celebrated practice to make women more desirable. The practice lasted more than one thousand years. It was said to be have been started by the last emperor of Nan Tang Dynasty (937-978 A.D), because his favored concubine had tiny feet. All other concubines and daughters of high ranking officials and nobles were encouraged to bind their feet as a kind of primitive cosmetic surgery. This art then flourished until the collapse of the Qing Dynasty in 1911. The art was seen as a twin of Chinese gardening and was equally enjoyed and celebrated among the intellectual classes. Natural "big feet" were considered inferior and marked a woman as belonging to the peasant class. (Source: Xin Hua)

Instead, for 2000 years, the elite class of nobles and emperors recreated the *land of peach blossoms* for pleasure, using ornaments and false rockeries, which became celebrated as the high art of gardening.

Ironically, this art accelerated the decline of the feudalist Chinese empire. In this sense, the art of gardening had no more relevance than the art of foot binding, which was so much appreciated by the emperors and nobles (*Figures 05a–07*).

The decaying art of gardening was recognized as a glorious tradition of Chinese national identity,

Figure 07 The false rockery in Liu Yuan, a typical Chinese garden in Suzhou, listed as a world heritage site: a highly abstract and fake Land of Peach Blossoms in a "bottle gourd", enjoyed by Chinese intellectual nobles. (Photo: Yu, K.J.)

Figures 08a,b The art of civic decoration is now flourishing but is an extension inherited from the decaying art of Chinese ornamental gardening. This is often combined with its Roman and Baroque counterparts. (Photos: Yu, K.J.)

Figures 09a-c Sacred Feng Shui trees in the formerly productive and picturesque countryside were dug out and transplanted to beautify the city. (Photo: Yu, K.J.)

and remains highly regarded by current western and Chinese scholars alike (*Figures 08a,b*).

In contrast, when building the cities of tomorrow, created by taking mature trees from the villages, diverting streams from farms, it is the actual vernacular of the *land of peach blossoms* that is being destroyed (*Figures 09a–10b*).

2 The Loss of the Land of Peach Blossoms: Challenges and Opportunities for Landscape Architecture

The role of agriculture has declined in China's urban-focused economy, along with the skills and the art of agricultural cultivation and stewardship.

This process began with the gardens of classical scholars from thousands of years ago, and has now spread to civic art and landscape design. Landscape design, once the art of the emperors, has descended into the realm of the trivial. Thousands of landscape architects compete for a tiny piece of land in the city. Simultaneously, the major rivers run dry and polluted, the underground water table continues to drop, and in the north, sand storms are affecting the area's arable land.

Each year, the processes of urbanization and materialization lure one percent (approximately 13 million people) of the Chinese population to

abandon their *land of peach blossoms* and rush into the city. This process has expanded urban boundaries and encroached on agricultural land (*Figures 11a,b*). The sacred *feng shui* forests have been cut and replaced with ornamental flowers. The graveyards of our ancestors have been leveled and their remains abandoned or removed to the planned cemetery. Ponds in front of the former villages have been filled, and whole villages have been wiped out and replaced with glorious, exotic, stylish walled communities. The meandering country roads are being replaced with six-lane motorways and a Baroque axis (Yu and Li, 2003, 2005).

Figure 10a The rendering of Beijing's CBD: the grandeur of tomorrow's city. (Source, Beijing Planning Bureau)

Figure 10b The actual CBD of Shanghai: A dentist's tool box
(Photo: Yu, K.J.)

11a Beijing 1984

11b Beijing 2004

Figures 11a,b The sprawl of Beijing over twenty years (1984–2004).

In the late 1980s and early 1990s, the Chinese began to work toward campaigns to beautify their cities, in line with the "new socialist countryside" campaign launched by the central Chinese government. This has placed Chinese landscape planning and design again at the forefront of an important precipice; there exists the danger of losing ecological integrity, cultural identity and historical heritage, while there also exists the great opportunity to create a new relationship between the land and the people in the current era.

Along with the processes of urbanization, the disappearance of the *land of peach blossoms* is obvious. The present era marks one of globalization and the spread of materialism. This has brought three major challenges and opportunities to landscape architecture in China.

2.1 The First Challenge: Can We Be Sustainable?

The first challenge is China's deteriorating environment and ecology. At the heart of this matter is Chinese survival and sustainability (*Figures 12a,b*).

Sixty-five percent of China's 1.3 billion people will, within 20 years, live in cities (the present rate is 40 percent). Two thirds of the 662 cities lack sufficient water and not a single river in the urban and suburban areas runs unpolluted. Thousands of dams crisscross nearly all rivers in China. More than ever, the general Chinese population is exposed to disastrous natural forces, as demonstrated by the numerous floods and droughts each year. The northern regions of China are in crisis because of desertification, where each year 3436 square kilometers of land become desert, a figure that is increasing each year. At present, the total area of desertification accounts for about 20 percent of the whole country, and each year about 5 billion tons of soil erodes into the ocean. (Jiang and Liu, 2004; Zhao, Huang, Yang and Guo; 2004). Statistics show that in the

Figure 12a Is this sustainable? China seen from a satellite. A "brown field" with little green, a land being torched by numerous natural and man-made disasters.

Figure 12b The land in China is just like an overladen horse (Drawing: Liu, Y.)

Figure 13 The chaotic land and misused landscape: the outskirts of Hangzhou, once known as the most beautiful city in China and a paradise on the earth. (Photo: Yu, K.J.)

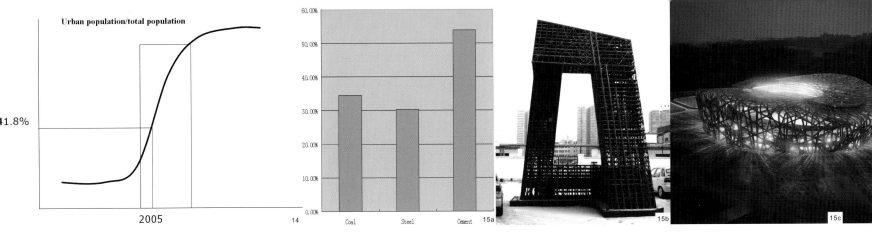

Figure 14 The predicted urban population in the next few years.

Figure 15a The material and energy consumption in China in terms of percentage of the total consumption worldwide. (Source: World Statistic Review of World Energy, 2005, BP, etc.)

Figures 15b–f Where does the steel and cement go?
(b) The CCTV tower with its 70 meters of overhang, is expected to consume 120,000 tons of steel, which is about 250 kilograms per square meter. This will cost almost 10 times as much as an ordinary office building in China.

past 50 years, 50 percent of the China's wetlands have disappeared, and 40 percent of the surviving wetlands have been polluted (Chen, Lu and Yong, 2004). The underground water level drops continuously. In Beijing for example, the underground water overuse is 110 percent, and each year the underground water level drops by one meter (*Figure 12a–20b*).

There are economic costs to this environmental destruction. While the GDP growth rate in the past 20 years is impressive in most Chinese cities, the annual loss caused by the environmental and ecological degradation is now between 7 and 20 percent of GDP. This is equal to, or even higher than the annual GDP growth (Guo 2004).

These are all by-products of China's double-digit GDP growth rate and the nation's speedy process of urbanization. One can only wonder if this is sustainable. Can China survive the rapid deterioration of the environment? What will this mean to the profession of landscape architecture, and how can landscape architecture position itself to play a role to meet such unprecedented challenges? This big picture leads us to argue that landscape architecture should be re-established as an art of survival, the emperor's art of land design and stewardship.

2.2 Who Are We? The Challenge of Cultural Identity

China's rapid and often chaotic socio-cultural transformation that started in the 1980s has led to a crisis in its national cultural identity. Traditionally, Chinese national identity was based on the feudalistic social and political order of the dynastic rulers. The architectural hallmarks of China, even in 2006, the items listed as national and world heritage sites, are products of

(c) The Beijing 2008 stadium, the "Bird's Nest", is expected to consume a total of 50 thousand tons of steel, about 500 kilograms per square meter, which is 17 times as much as that used in building the Sydney Olympic stadium which was considered outrageously expensive at the time;

(d) Square paving, one of the typical out-of-scale urban squares being built in almost every Chinese city;
(e&f) River channelizing and damming: few of the rivers across China have not been channelized with concrete and dammed. The Three Gorges alone consumed 16 million cubic meters of concrete. (Photos: Yu, K.J.)

Figures 16a,b Cars in the water and boats on the ground: a waterlogged street in Beijing after a storm, while at the same time, the former wetland in the Grand View Garden is dry. All of the storm water was drained through pipes to the ocean while Beijing used more than its allotted underground water. This caused natural wetland to dry up and has made the land sink by 1 meter each year. (a Source: Xin Hua; b Photo: Yu, K.J.)

Figures 17a–c Sand storm in Beijing and across northern China. (Source: Xin Hua)

feudalism, the imperial era, and the official scholarly culture. While past achievements cannot be denied, it is necessary to ask whether this style represents national Chinese cultural identity in 2006 (*Figures 21–25e*).

This identity crisis is particularly obvious in the area of urban design. When a French designer places his own masterpiece (the National Grand Opera House) into the center of China's capital to realize his own dream, or when the majestic but "dysfunctional" Central TV Tower is built only for the "power to bewitch" (Daniel Burnham), designers must question what is really being displayed to the rest of the world? Torn between its own imperial past and today's westernization, what is China's identity? These are important, broader questions for China's landscape architects to consider.

2.3 Why We are Living: The Death of Gods

The third challenge is the loss of the spiritual homeland, where the soul rests and life is devoted to finding meaning.

My grandmother told me that when a tree grows old, it becomes a spirit, and that some spirits will inhabit the old trees. It has been said that the same is true of the fish, snakes, birds, and other animals. An old rock beside a village becomes a spirit as do streams, ponds, hills and the land itself. Our parents built temples in which to shelter and worship ancestors, the wise men of the past, and the religious spirits who safeguarded welfare. It was once believed that these spirits protected earthly life, and that the future would depend on their judgment. Such spirits gave meaning to life (*Figures 26a,b*).

The jobs of 40 million farmers have been lost in recent years, a figure that increases annually by two million. Where do the landless farmers

Figure 18 New developments take over productive land. (Photo: Yu, K.J.)

Figure 19a&b The Dragon King (the symbol of floods) tamed: trying to control the floods and tides using concrete and heavy engineering projects is an ugly folly. Even Hainan Island, China's paradise, is surrounded with a high concrete dike. (Photos: Yu, K.J.)

Figures 20a,b Cities are decorated with expensive and intensively maintained exotic ornamental plants, and the native vegetation is completely wiped out because it is ordinary looking and not seen as exotic. (Photo: Yu, K.J.)

belong and what is their spiritual homeland? The bankruptcy of the former state-owned factories has left more than 21 million workers jobless. How much will they suffer spiritually because they were conditioned to "regard the factory as their home"? (*Figures 27a–28b*)

The trend toward materialism has taken over China at a rapid rate, just as it has in other regions around the world. Every piece of land and all the elements in the landscape have been inhabited by various spirits where ancestors have been buried. These plains have been taken over by real-estate development. The *Dragon Hills*, or the

sacred hills, that secured numerous villages in rural China have been bulldozed. Meaningful and sacred streams and ponds that once shielded villages have been filled in or channeled in the name of flood control. Old camphor trees that house tree spirits have been pruned and sold to beautify city boulevards. Landscapes have become commercialized. Gradually, the spiritual connection to the land and to the world beyond this earthly one has been lost (*Figures 29 a–c*).

It is certainly a nostalgic attitude to believe that the ideal agricultural landscape will be the model for everyday living, and it is naive to believe that

Figure 21 The dilemma of identity: torn between its own imperial past and today's westernization, what is China's identity? (Courtesy Lu, J.L.)

Figure 22 In feudal China, identity was not a problem (Drawing: Allom, T.)

Figure 23a&b Chinese cities now feature European Baroque landscapes with Roman arches. (Photos: Yu, K.J.)

Figures 24a,b Emperor Qin Sihuang in his imperial yellow robe with his monumental army of clay warriors. (Courtesy Lu, J.L.)

Figures 25a–c Emperor Qin Sihuang now wears a western suit. Perhaps this explains why Beijing's so called "modern" flavored CCTV tower and National Grand Opera House, (designed by Dutch architect Rem Koolhaas and French architect Paul Andreu respectively) were selected by their Chinese clients. (Courtesy Lu, J.L.)

the *land of peach blossoms* can be regained and kept in the industrialized, motorized, and globally connected society. A new type of *land of peach blossoms* must be explored and created, and it is to this mission that the profession of landscape architecture fits at the right time and at the right place. But how can this be achieved? How can landscape architecture assume the role to protect and rebuild such material and spiritual connections through the design of the physical environment? This is perhaps the most challenging question of all.

3 Recreating the *Land of Peach Blossoms* in a New Era: The Mission of Contemporary Landscape Architecture

3.1 What is the Mission?

In facing environmental and ecological degradation, a loss of cultural identity and the erosion of spiritual connection to the land, the mission of contemporary landscape architecture is to bring together again nature, people and the spirits, to create a new *land of peach blossoms* in the urbanized, global, and industrialized era.

3.2 Why Landscape Architecture?

Landscape architecture can play a major role in the mission to rebuild the *land of peach blossoms* because it is a medium upon which various natural, cultural, and spiritual processes interact. This creates a workable link to gather and harmonize nature, people, and spiritual processes. Prominent naturalist and biologist Edward Wilson once commented that, "In the expanding enterprise, landscape design will play a decisive role. Where the environment has been mostly humanized, biological diversity can still be sustained at high levels by the ingenious

Figure 26a A family meeting in an ancestral worship hall: this was once a spiritual place for Chinese people. (Photo: Yu, K.J.)

Figure 26b A family gathered in front of an ancestral graveyard to pay tribute to their ancestors: a spiritual link to the family and the land. (Photo: Yu, K.J.)

Figures 27a&b "Where is my home?" Farmers lose their homes, their houses torn down for urban development, their fields reclaimed. Now they flood the cities looking for jobs and shelter. (Photo: Yu, K.J.)

Figures 28a,b *"Where is my home?" The bankruptcy of former state owned factories leads to massive redundancies. (Photos: Yu, K.J.)*

Figure s27c,d "I want go home": A young country girl finds a job in the city but misses her country home(Photo: Li, J.K.), just like an old tree uprooted and transplanted to an unfamiliar place. (Photos, Yu, K.J.)

placement of woodlots, hedgerows, watersheds, reservoirs, and artificial ponds and lakes. Master plans will meld not just economic efficiency and beauty, but also the preservation of the species and the race." (Wilson 1992, page 317).

Landscape refers here not only to the issue of the environment and ecology but also to the mood of the entire nation, to its sense of identity, and its cultural bearings (Girot, 1999). Landscape provides a foundation for connection, for home, and for belonging (Corner, 1999). Landscape architecture is possibly the most legitimate profession among those dealing with the physical environment to work toward recovering cultural identity and rebuilding the spiritual connection between people and their land. The strength of landscape architecture lies in its intrinsic association with the natural systems and its roots in agricultural traditions, matching local practices and variegated across thousands of years of evolution.

It strengthens the motto that the best way to think globally is to act locally. Landscape architecture is the most workable scale for local action. Therefore, it is legitimate to argue that landscape architecture is a promising profession, and in China it is the right time to take on the mission of recreating the *land of peach blossoms*. Or to quote Patrick A Miller at the 2005 ASLA conference, "it is an opportune time to become a landscape architect".

3.3 How and Where: Strategies and Approaches

How should landscape architecture as a profession respond to these challenges and what principles should landscape architecture adopt to prepare for a leading role to bring together the land, people, and spirits?

Firstly, landscape design should harmonize with nature, its processes, patterns and the sustainable welfare of humanity. Landscape design should be practiced with people in mind, while at the same time considering human culture and identity. Landscape architecture should also be designed with spirits in mind, connecting the land and the people as individuals, as well as in terms of family and social groups. These three principles of land, people, and spirits require landscape architecture to adjust its own position and value.

Secondly, it is also about who are we and where we come from. In turn, this determines what we will become in the future, what we should value, that which determines where and what kind of landscape is being preserved and created. As such, it is necessary to address the three following points.

28b

29a

Grand House On Wealth Boulevard At CBD

CBD 财富大道 人文新邸
诚邀阁下莅临CLUB级的接待中心

29b

29c

Figures 29a–c Materialism prevails: Buddha was worshiped for his power to offer wealth. Images of luxury items and swanky villas are omnipresent. Is this the new "Chinese dream"? (Photos: Yu, K.J; Source, Real Estate Review, 2005.)

3.3.1 Recovering Landscape Architecture as the Art of Survival

First and foremost, if landscape architecture is to establish itself as a profession that safeguards humanity and brings together the land, the people, and the spirit, its origins must be reconsidered. Its roots must be recovered as the regal lord's art of survival, land design, and land stewardship, and not as an art of entertaining and gardening. McHarg has expressed the role of the architect as a means of survival thus: "We told you so; you've got to listen to us because we're landscape architects. We're going to tell you thereafter where to live and how to live there. Where to live and where not to live. That's what landscape architecture and regional planning is all about. Don't ask us about your garden. Don't ask us about your bloody flowers. Don't ask us about

your dying trees. You can do something quite vulgar with all of them. We are going to talk to you about survival." (Miller and Pardal, 1992)

More than half a century ago, educator and landscape architect, Hideo Sasaki commented that, "the profession of landscape architecture stands at a critical fork in the road. One fork leads to a significant field of endeavor contributing to the betterment of the human environment, while the other points to a subordinate field of superficial embellishment." Unfortunately, except for some rare cases, landscape architecture in the past decade has been biased toward "a subordinate field of superficial embellishment". We could have taken one more important role in some of

the most pressing environmental issues including flood control and water management, the protection of biodiversity and cultural heritage, urbanization, and land resources management (*Figures 30a–34b*).

One of the most important reasons for landscape architecture's weakness in addressing major environmental issues is that landscape architecture, as a profession, is still associated with the ancient tradition of gardening. The rich heritage and overwhelming literature about gardening and garden art did not help landscape architecture emerge as a modern discipline. It is time to declare that landscape architecture is not a direct descendent of garden art, but a descendent of the survival skills of our ancestors who had to endure a changeable environment, ensuring a safe place away from floods and enemies, while

21

Figure 31a The art of survival: Lin Qu in China. A weir was built more than 2000 years ago and is still in use. It makes friends with natural forces and makes it possible to harness the powerful force of nature. (Photo: Unknown)

Figure 31b The art of survival getting lost in the engineering of fighting against nature: the Three Gorges dam cuts across the largest river in China. (Source: Xin Hua)

Figures 30a–c Natural disasters are closing in on the massive populations of our modern societies (the Southeast Asia tsunami in 2004 and the Katrina disaster in New Orleans in 2005). (Source: Xin Hua)

surviving by leveling the land, planting and irrigating crops, and saving water and other resources for sustaining the family and the people. Landscape architecture works on a larger and more significant scale than the field of garden arts.

The landscape needs to be recovered (Corner, 1999) and the profession of landscape architecture needs to be recovered. This suggests that more international efforts are required to give landscape architecture more publicity through illustrative cases and to demonstrate how landscape architecture plays the leading role in dealing with the big environmental and survival issues.

3.3.2 Valuing the Vernacular: Back to the Authentic Relationship of Land and People

By vernacular, I mean the common and everyday, as opposed to the grand and exotic. Cultural identity and spiritual connection can be regained only if we value the culture of the common people, their life and their daily needs, as well as value the common things that are authentic to the land under foot.

Since the appearance of the first imperial and intellectual gardens in China, as well as in other countries, landscaping and gardening had become indulgent in creating the exotic and the grand, and being different from the common landscape and living environment. This can be well illustrated by the Chinese Imperial Garden of Shanglin Yuan of more than 2000 years ago, which features exotic plants and animal species. Another example is the intellectual gardens of South China's Souzhou, which represented spectacular and exotic scenic spots using rocks and water, and the imperial Grand View Gardens of the 17th century, which was a collection of gardens from South China. In this sense, there is virtually no difference to western culture, as reflected in the English gardens that included exotic ornamental species from China and Versailles, that were created as a paradise in a sea of "chaotic vernacular landscapes".

The overwhelming *Beautiful Cities* movement in China, as inherited from that of the United States, also has its own "city gardens" origin, but is an extension of this decorative cosmetic and exotic search. For a long time, indeed more than 2000 years, the art of landscaping has lost its way in searching for senseless style, meaningless form

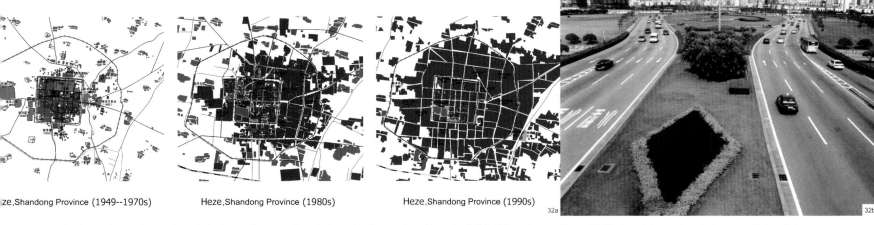

Heze,Shandong Province (1949--1970s)   Heze,Shandong Province (1980s)   Heze,Shandong Province (1990s)   32a

32b

Figure 32a The art of survival getting lost: the landscape changes at Heze city located in the waterlogged lower land of the Yellow River Valley. Historically, lot ponds were designed and preserved in the city to contain storm water so that waterlogging could be avoided. The urbanization process in recent decades totally ignored this art of survival and city design and the ponds in the city were filled and built on, which caused serious waterlogging. (Source, Graduate School of Landscape Archtecture, Peking University)

Figure 32b The loss of the art of survival: the art of urban design for living became the art of decoration: Shenzhen in south China. (Photo: Yu, K.J.)

and exotic grandeur. Landscape gardening has for a long time been limited to the elite class, including the city dwellers, who have not cared about the survival of the common people in the continuous struggle with flood and drought.

In China, only recently has it been found that it is the elite class themselves who are now suffering, perhaps no less than the farmers, from the nation's deteriorating environment. The skills of survival reflect the authentic relationship between the land and the people, and it is this authentic relationship that gives the culture and the people its identity. It is therefore critical for landscape architecture to go back to the land, go back to the vernacular relationship, to recover survival skills in dealing with flood, drought, soil erosion, making fields, and food production, and more broadly to regain its cultural identity.

3.3.3 Landscape Architecture Leading the Way: The Negative Approach—Landscape as Infrastructure for Urban Development

How landscape changes is related to the issue of time. The processes of urbanization and globalization occur rapidly and overwhelmingly, and a "negative" approach should be taken

against the conventional development planning approach. By negative, it is meant that landscape architects and planners should lead the way in urban development by identifying and designing a landscape infrastructure that is critical in safeguarding the ecological processes, and the cultural heritages that give us our cultural identity and feed the spiritual needs, before the development plan evolves.

Time in the conventional model of urbanization is visualized in the concentric annual sprawl. For a long time, greenbelts and green wedges were seen as landscape structures to stop and prevent such sprawl, and they were pre-designed in the comprehensive master plan. Current evidence based on the United States (for example, the Washington DC region), as well as Chinese examples, show that these greenbelt and wedge dreams have failed. Some of the major reasons that the greenbelt and green wedge have failed to prevent urban sprawl include:

1 The artificial planning and the lack of an intrinsic relationship between the green elements and the living earth system;

2 A lack of usage by the residents, due to their inaccessibility and lack of connectivity between green space and housing projects;

3 Green wedges usually function only as barriers to stop urban sprawl processes, and offer a lack of integration of the various functions, such as flood control, recreational use, heritage protection, and habitat protections;

4 They quickly become development opportunities when peripheral pressures increase;

5 They are impossible to administer and safeguard in a metropolitan region that is fragmented into many local governments, cutting across greenbelt and wedge jurisdictions.

The search continues for a more differentiated, fine-grained ecological integration model that can be envisioned, implemented, and managed at all scales. As a consequence, the ecological planning approach has risen to prominence again, typically under the flag of the McHarg Layer model, which attempts to provide land use planning on a sound ecological basis.

23

Figure 33a The art of survival: a settlement carefully sits on the bank of a meandering stream. (Photo: Yu, K.J.)

Figure 33b The loss of the art of survival: a living stream was channelized for flood control but completely destroyed its life. (Photo: Yu, K.J.)

Figures 34a,b The vernacular landscape and ordinary landscape for survival. (Photo: Yu, K.J.)

Under this framework, time is visualized as a line that links, and as a tool that enables understanding, and integrates vertically different layers of physical, natural, and cultural processes. These include the earliest geological processes, soil processes, vegetation processes, and finally leaves on top the most recent layer of cultural processes. It is a vision of progress of natural evolution based on the intrinsic values of a specific site on the earth. The core for this model of ecological planning is that what fits best can plan urban development. With the maximum fitting of the land use pattern to the intrinsic values on the earth, the best development pattern can be achieved.

These two models, namely the conventional urban growth model and the ecological planning model, are incompatible. One of the obvious reasons for this incompatibility is that the conventional urban growth is often a horizontal process, while the ecological suitability analysis is essentially a vertical process. The green space based on the layering model not only protects the horizontal ecological processes, such as species movement in the system, it may actually become attractive for intensive urban development due to the higher economic value surrounding this greenbelt, which may eventually be encroached upon by development.

The development of landscape ecology, which focuses on landscape patterns, horizontal processes and change, provides us with the fundamentals to develop green infrastructure that can be used to integrate the horizontal processes of urban development with ecological protection. This is a new ecological planning model in which time can be visualized as a multi-scaled ecological infrastructure, or landscape security pattern (Yu, 1996), that safeguards the various ecological, cultural and spiritual processes across the landscape, and provides ecosystems services for the sustainability of a region and a city such as water and flood processes, biodiversity protection and species flow, and recreation.

At a large scale, the ecological infrastructure is represented as a permanent regional landscape of flood prevention, ecological networks, heritage corridors and recreational corridors, which are to be planned for protection and used to define the urban growth pattern and city form.

At the intermediate scale, the regional ecological infrastructure is to be integrated into the interior urban structure, and become the urban green space system that integrates various functions such as commuting, cycling, heritage protection and recreational activities.

At the small scale, the ecological infrastructure is to be used as the defining structure for urban land development, and can be used to guide the site-specific design.

This landscape infrastructure becomes an integrated medium of various processes, bringing together nature, people and their spirit. It is the efficient landscape security pattern to safeguard ecological and environmental integrity, cultural identity, and to provide for people's spiritual needs.

34b

In order to do that, landscape architecture must break with the art of gardening, and return to the vernacular landscape and people, and must lead the process of urban development by preserving and integrating cultural and ecological landscapes into the infrastructure.

Summary

For thousands of years, people struggled with natural forces to survive, and as a result created a landscape that reflected the balanced relationship between man and nature, and that recorded people's hardship and happiness. The knowledge and skills associated with this authentic relationship sustain people for generation after generation, give people their identity, and provide their lives with meaning. Their knowledge and skills make up the essence of the profession called landscape architecture. This art of survival, however, has been buried and submerged in the high art of gardening, which only reflects a false relationship between the land and people.

At the new era, the balance between man and nature has been broken again, and the survival of humanity has again become critical so that a new, harmonious relationship must be built. This is the opportunity for landscape architecture to recover its role as an art of survival, and to take the position to recreate a new type of *land of peach blossoms*, that sustains humanity, gives people their identity, and makes their life meaningful.

References

Chen Kelin, Lu Yong, Zhang Xiaohong, 2004, No Water Without Wetland, in: China Environment and Development Review, 296–309, Social Sciences Documentation Publishing House

Corner, James, 1999, Recovering Landscape as a Critical Cultural Practice, in: James, Corner (editor), Recovering Landscape: Essays in Contemporary Landscape Architecture, Princeton Architectural Press

Fajardo, Martha, 2005, Forward, in Yu, K-J. and D-H Li (editors), Landscape Architecture: Profession and Education, in: The China Architectural Industry Press, Beijing, China, 1–6

Girot, Christophe, 1999, Four Trace Concepts in Landscape Architecture, in: James, Corner (editor), Recovering Landscape: Essays in Contemporary Landscape Architecture. Princeton Architectural Press, 59–67

Guo Xiaomin, The Economic Cost of Environmental Pollution and Ecological Deterioration, in: China Environment And Development Review, 53–71. Social Sciences Documentation Publishing House

Jiang Gaoming, Liu Meizhen, 2004, Sand Storm, China Environment and Development Review, 310–322, Social Sciences Documentation Publishing House

Miller E.L. and Pardal, S., 1992, The Classic McHarg, An Interview, Published by CESUR, Technical University of Lisbon

Padua, Mary G., 2003, Industrial Strength– Zhongshan Shipyard Park: At a Former Shipyard, a Park Design Breaks with Convention to Honor China's Recent Past, Landscape Architecture, June, 76–85, 105–107

Wilson, O. Edward, 1992, The Diversity of Life, The Belknap Press of Harvard University Press, Cambridge

Yu, K-J and Li, D-H, 2003, Road to Urban Landscape, The Chinese Architectural Industry Press (In Chinese)

Yu, K-J and Li, D-H, and Liu, H-L, 2005, The Negative Approach, The Chinese Architectural Industry Press (In Chinese)

Yu, K-J, 1996, Security Patterns and Surface Model in Landscape Planning. Landscape and Urban Planning, 36 (5) 1–17

Zhao Jingxing, Huang Ping, Yang Chaofei, Guo Xiaomin, 2004, Situation of China's Environment and Development, in China Environment and Development Review, Vol. 2, 23–50, Social Sciences Documentation Publishing House

1.2 Seeking the Deity of the Land

Kongjian Yu, ASLA

Dean and Professor, The Graduate School of Landscape Architecture, Peking University and President, Turenscape, Beijing, China

"We live in modern times. Unlike the pre-modern era when the farmers in the fields and the fisherman by the sea were attuned to mother nature, we have lost touch with, and no longer have the opportunity to feel her breath and comprehend her feelings. As a result, we completely ignore the many clues she sent to us prior to a great disaster (Yu)".

"If we respected heaven like our own father, and loved the earth like our own mother, heaven and the earth would nurture us like their own beloved children. However, if we betrayed heaven, abused the earth, and behaved willfully, we would face never-ending disasters and dig our own graves" (*Respect Heaven and Earth*, Chien Kun Vol. 4, 2005).

In the following article, Professor Yu explores a similar subject from an academic perspective where he arrives at alarming, in-depth conclusions. The essay provides a profound response and a call to action. People should be ashamed of the ruthless behavior that has damaged and poisoned mother earth. This article was written after the tsunami disaster in the Indian Ocean, but before the Katrina disaster in New Orleans. The Katrina disaster was caused by the "100-year-flood" and the failure of concrete levees that artificially protected the city. These are his warnings.

Chien Kun magazine has advocated the ideal of people living in harmony with heaven and earth. In *Home Planet Volume 5*, the dire consequences of the ecosystem's deterioration were pointed out, and it was warned that the human race may be facing obliterating disasters and must start action to save the earth. Coincidentally, these warnings have echoed Dr Yu's warning. It is hoped that more people can awaken to the severity of ecological crisis. The following are excerpts taken from this article.

(Editor of *Chien Kun*, Vol. 7/2006: 36–45)

1.2.1 Catastrophe in *Paradise*

The tsunami disaster in 2004 led to extensive worldwide discussion that covered many dimensions including science, religion, and philosophy.

As a civil planner and a landscape architect, the main goal of landscape planning and design is to coordinate the relationship between humans and the land. Therefore, this article concentrates on this aspect, and is based on the notion that the disaster happened in a constructed "paradise". Beautiful gardens and luxurious hotels were turned into rubble in a few moments.

Nearly 300,000 lives, including many educated people who were equipped with modern scientific knowledge were taken. Conversely, the pre-modern local tribes who lived on remote islands survived the disaster free from harm. Scientists detected the earthquakes and with their scientific knowledge, predicted that tsunamis would follow, yet these people were still not spared from death.

This tsunami disaster was a serious warning to think about the ecological safety of the modern country and the cities in today's trend of hyper-urbanization.

Contemplation 1

The land's ecological safety is the first priority. Several thousand years of technological development has not been able to lessen the threat of natural disasters. Forests, beaches, rivers, and cities are susceptible to disasters. Many civilizations in human history were suddenly eliminated by natural disaster. The development of Chinese civilization, in a certain sense, presents a history that recognises and copes with natural disaster. Historians believe that the formation of the first Chinese dynasty, the Xia, was mainly due to the necessity to organize a large labor force to deal with flooding.

Aside from the problem of overpopulation, the biggest challenge facing modern China is the ecological security of the country. Traditional family ethics and western religious ethics were overcome to successfully resolve the problem of overpopulation. It must be asked: what will become the "Deity" over the land that can provide ecological safety for this overburdened earth?

Contemplation 2

The "Superman" mentality and the world of virtual reality has caused disasters to occur.

Facing the mortality of 300,000 people and also the miraculous survival of the pre-modern local communities, one cannot help but ask whether we have we progressed or regressed in dealing with natural disasters.

In the early days of factories when we built with machines, we strengthened and extended our bodies. By developing computers and information technology, we have expanded our brains. We have made ourselves into 'Supermen'. Contemporary technology has forced us to live in a highly abstract world.

Concrete levees designed to withstand a 100-year flood created livable cities. However, these artificial constructions created visual and physical barriers that blocked any sense of the flood's tidal flow, be it high or low. The water flow may be channeled and controlled, yet sight of its source has been lost and with it, the organisms that live in it. Mountains are flattened and valleys are filled, and as a consequence, any concept of the natural topography of the landscape is lost. More and more, we have become strangers to nature. Unlike pre-modern times when the farmers worked in the field and fishermen worked with the sea, there is no longer an opportunity to feel the breath of mother nature, and comprehend her feelings. As a result, the clues she often delivers right before a great disaster strikes are ignored.

Creating an urban society that can coexist with the natural system so that modern city-dwellers can sense nature is fundamental to the creation of a new and harmonious relationship between humans and the land.

Humans have an inherent awe and love for mother nature. For millions of years, she has brought disasters to humans and with them, ensured long-lasting memories. Simultaneously, she bestows food and shelter. As part of mother nature's world, humankind has developed a kinship with the earth as part of a deeply imbedded ethos. It is the basis for an inherent sensitivity towards the potential fortune and misfortune of the land around us, and for appreciating its beauty. If there is an over-dependency on modern technology, our sensitivity and value system toward mother nature, that evolved over tens of millions of years, will deteriorate and be lost forever. The overwhelming surrender to modern high technology will begin the destruction of the species. It is critical to take action and revive our understanding of mother nature, and to find a balance between the scientific and technological knowledge of everyday life.

Contemplation 3

Re-acquainting ourselves with the value of cultural heritage is another key issue. The pre-modern local communities survived the tsunami disaster by their demonstration of the value of native cultural heritage. Traditional local cultural heritage includes the traditions of ancestors, their customs, and mythologies. Physical manifestations are the products of local indigenous tribes and their symbiotic relationship with the land, a system that has developed over many generations. The preservation of these traditions is vitally important and demands careful attention.

At the same time, it is important to recognize the fact that in an age of rapid urbanization, with the resulting over-population and limited resources, it cannot be expected that the answers will be provided from the sustained knowledge of the pre-modern indigenous tribes. The modern age cries out for a new "Deity" for leadership through such complex times.

Contemplation 4

What is the purpose of scientific technology? How can it sustain the lives of 1.3 billion people in China? The current strategy for the environmental safety of the land and the cities is to create artificial constructions that fight against nature. An examination of the recent history of flooding in China shows that the most severe damage resulted from our over-reliance on using products of scientific technology to fight a persistent and lengthy battle with nature. For example, the flooding that has resulted from the collapse of levees and dams.

Science seemed to bear no responsibility for the consequences of the Indian Ocean tsunami disaster. The scientists detected the earthquakes and advised that tsunamis would follow. Unfortunately, the communication delivery system was not effective, because of the lack of advancement of communication systems in the affected under-developed areas. A comprehensive program is required to convey information in a timely manner.

During the pre-scientific age, religion and ethics were firmly built into human moral principles and behavior. All natural phenomena were treated as signs of either "fortune" or "misfortune". For instance, ancient Chinese *feng shui* describes curved and continuous rivers as "fortunate", and good for habitation. Modern day ecological studies confirm that naturally curved rivers help to reduce the force of flooding and damage. Yet today, our engineered defense against flooding is to build a dam, realign and channel rivers into rectilinear forms, thus eliminating the curved forms. Scientific knowledge has not helped us to wisely utilize, adapt, and reform nature. Adversely, we use this knowledge in the most superficial and limited sense.

In summary, the relationship between humans and the earth should not be a contentious one, full of struggle, but should strive for "harmony". Scientific technology should not be used to create "Supermen" to fight nature but coordinate the relationship between humans and mother nature. Utilizing science should incorporate ethics so it can become the angel that propagates beauty. Otherwise, it will only become a negative and destructive force that undermines the human race.

1.2.2 Laying Down the Knife That Slew the Land "Goddess": Reconstructing Ecological Ethics.

During the 1999 World Architecture Congress, Professor Wu Liang Yong stated, "Our time is the age of great development and great destruction".

Not only has the ancestors' heritage of prominently promoting harmony between humans and nature (the poetic cultural landscape) been abandoned, but lessons provided by urban development in western countries have not been learnt using scientific theories and methodologies that deal with the relationship between humans and the land. The natural system of the earth has suffered different degrees of destruction throughout the urbanization process.

During the past two decades, modern urban construction in China has largely been paid for with the accumulation of enormous waste and the sacrifice of the health and safety of the natural system. Wise planning and design could have prevented this nation-wide destruction, including:

1 The fragmentation of the land, the disorganized expansion of cities, freeways and road system that pay no consideration to the environment. A variety of land developments, construction and irrigation practices have all contributed to the non contiguous natural terrain. As a result, the continuity and integrity of the natural process have been severely damaged.

2 Handicapped water systems. Watershed and natural drainage systems have been severely compromised. Once the product of the combined efforts of humans and natural process working together over thousands of years, it is now subject to engineering practices that involve the underground burial of river channels, realignment and artificial channeling, and the destruction of wetlands.

3 The disappearance of bio-habitats. The natural lands have disappeared; riverbeds and vegetation have been replaced by levees and "beautification" planting. Trees used to fence farmlands and roadside trees have been cut down for road expansion projects. The cultural landscape and bio-habitats around ponds, bushes near residences, cemeteries, and trees planted for good *feng shui*, are disappearing at an alarming rate.

The expansion of cities and the development of infrastructures are necessary in this modern era. However, the land is limited, and it must be remembered that the natural system has its own structure. Coordinating the relationship between cities and nature is by no means a matter of "quantity". It is, more importantly, a matter of space structuring and "quality". This means that an approach should be taken that considers careful scientific land-design processes. This will greatly reduce the interference that city building and the establishment of infrastructure impose upon the ecosystem. These actions can help avoid destruction. Creating environmental consciousness, ethics and responsibility are the key to accomplishing this.

1.2.3 The Power of "Superman" Cannot Replace the Ecological Aspects of the Natural System

Many kinds of physical and chemical compounds have been invented to combat biological and non-biological pathogens that can eliminate anything that harms our bodies. The effect has been the constant weakening of the immune system. The WHO (World Health Organization) has warned repeatedly that the newest strain of viral influenza could kill tens of millions of people. The scientific method of preparing for the disease is to strengthen bodies and build up our immune systems.

The same situation applies to cities. All kinds of man-made construction projects have been undertaken to protect cities from the destructive forces of nature. The massive engineering structures created by humans are not only strikingly expensive, they also create barriers between cities and nature. Consequently, the natural balance of the water system has been destroyed, the power of floods grows ever stronger, and rainwater is a rare natural resource that is dumped into the ocean.

The earth is a living "Goddess"; not only does she provide, she also digests and self-purifies, and she regulates all sorts of abundances and deficiencies. However, during the planning of cities and their construction, there has been a failure to comprehend the dynamic processes of nature. Furthermore, the "Land Goddess" has been most cruelly destroyed and poisoned, shattering her functionality. Her body (farmlands, grasslands, and fields of the earth) has been dismembered; her bones and muscles (the mountains of the earth) have been ruined; her kidneys (the wetlands system) have been damaged; her circulatory system and veins (the river systems) blocked; and her lungs (forests and bio-habitats) have been poisoned. A small snow or rainstorm will have the power to paralyze the entire city of Beijing. A flu virus can mutate into SARS and mortally threaten the country's numerous cities.

The strength and resistance of city dwellers, and their immunity to natural disasters should be increased, not by modern technology, but by allowing the natural system to fully perform its ecological functions, and carry out its wonders. This is a positive approach toward building, and in this way the immunity of all the living systems of the land can be strengthened.

1.2.4 Rebuilding the Elegance and Beauty of Landscape; Constructing an Eco-safe Framework Through "Reverse Planning"

In 1962, landscape architect and environmental planning pioneer Ian McHarg led his students to study the eastern seaboard of the United States. The students were amazed by the wealthy population's ignorance, locating their expensive homes within a dangerous tidal zone. McHarg warned these self-assured people to relocate out of the zone as soon as possible to avoid disaster. Regrettably, his warnings were ignored and strong tidal waves destroyed these handsome houses only a few months later.

McHarg pleaded for people to listen to landscape architects who are able to select feasible locations for habitation. "This is the real essence of landscape planning and regional planning. We are trying to educate you about survival, and ways to deal with the force of nature". From the tsunami disaster in the Indian Ocean, history has taught that sometimes it repeats itself, which is an important lesson.

Recently, an Australian professor who has worked in Indonesia on the reconstruction of the region after the tsunami advised that many hotels and towns suffered such extensive damage because they were subject to a number of classical planning errors—in particular, the designs did not follow the laws of nature.

This planet has enough space to sustain the human species. However, often cities have been located and built in the wrong places due to poor methodology. Almost all coastal and riverside cities compete with nature by increasing the height of levees to control flooding. If a disaster had not struck for 100 years, it could possibly happen in the 101st year. If a disaster has a history of only once in 500 years, it does not imply that it cannot, or will not, occur tomorrow. If a city has been built in the wrong place, it doesn't matter how pretty it is, it can vanish overnight. It happened at the *La Family Ruin* in China 4000 years ago. The same thing happened to the ancient Roman city of Pompeii. The tsunami disaster of the Indian Ocean demonstrated the wrath of mother nature.

The fundamental solution is to respect the natural process of the earth. Using scientific analysis of the natural processes and the disaster processes, a landscape security pattern and ecological infrastructure can be developed, and the living systems of the land can be maintained.

General city building processes must be modified. Nature's process must be worked with to create safe and secure habitats for society. The design and construction of cities can be based on better informed choices. Cities of the past were sliding toward disaster on a dangerous trail, but the opportunity exists in the urbanization process to adjust the human–land relationship. The

resources to reverse the course of urban development and planning are available, so it is necessary to perform "reverse-engineering". First, it is necessary to establish an ecological infrastructure and a landscape security framework and to use this framework to define the plans for urban development. Otherwise, the future is open to more disasters.

1.2.5 With the Resurrection of the "Deity", Humanity Can Survive for Generations to Come

During a time of urbanization and the rapid deterioration of the environment in the United States, McHarg lamented as to why some natural lands in the metropolitan areas could not be saved so that nature could provide its free services for the people. He questioned why highly productive farms don't feature in cities to feed those in need. In the same way, is it not possible to utilize the natural systems to construct open spaces in the cities, so the city-dwellers can enjoy them for generations? Why do people reside in places where they shouldn't? And finally, why are the natural process and patterns to design our homes not adhered to rather than methodologies that constantly clash with nature?

According to a Chinese saying, "A person put into a desperate situation will be forced to find a way to survive". After going through "Superman" arrogance, an over-reliance on technology, and having a lack of faith in the industrial age, the death of the "Goddess" of the land, and the onslaught of a never-ending cycle of disasters, the new era of modern science must bring about the revitalization and reincarnation of the "Goddess".

Due to their ignorance and fear of nature, humans have created the "divinities" of the pre-scientific age. These divinities or deities were highly fearful of nature and, at the same time, sacred beyond approach. However, in today's highly scientific and technologically advanced age, it seems necessary to befriend a "Deity", which can be communicated with, respected, and yet still be approachable. Mother nature, with her natural processes and laws, is respected because of her unlimited power. She is amiable because of her open-mindedness and generosity. Simultaneously, she grows weak and deserves our sympathy.

Compared with the ignorant pre-scientific society's superstition toward "divinity", a more self-confident approach should be expected today. Now that the natural processes are fully understood via scientific knowledge (rather than a unilateral self-centered arrogance), there should now be a confidence. There is no reason for the human race to overpower nature for the sake of survival. Nature can actually foster healthier lives. Knowledge and respect for the human–land relationship can eventually become a new form of land ethics. Love and respect for natural processes and frameworks is fundamental for these new ethics. They should be codified and become part of the legal system, and regulate behavior toward the land.

In conclusion, the "deities" of the pre-scientific age cannot assure the eco-safety of the modern urbanites, nor can the industrial "Superman" protect from natural disasters. The integration of scientific knowledge and the new ethics of the land can help to create the moment for the coming of the modern "Deity", who can guide planning efforts to develop an ecologically safe environment.

(This article was first published in Chinese in *China Youth Daily*, February 23, 2005; and the Selective English version translated by Y.C. Huang was published in Chien Kun, Vol. 7/2006: 36–45, New York, USA).

1.3 Vernacular Cities and Vernacular Landscapes

The Legacy of the May 4th Movement in Chinese Landscape Architecture

Kongjian Yu, ASLA

Dean and Professor, The Graduate School of Landscape Architecture, Peking University and President, Turenscape, Beijing, China

Birgit Linder of the The Chinese University of Hong Kong, Hong Kong

At the moment light versus dark, life versus death and the past versus the future, I provide this patch of wild grass as evidence for all, friends and enemies, humans and beasts, the loved and the unloved.
Lu Xun, Ye Cao (Wild Grass)

Abstract

More than 80 years after the May 4th Movement, China again faces an identity crisis in its move toward globalization. The human–land relationship particularly reflects this crisis. Still, the Chinese landscape and urban design vacillate between often "dysfunctional" imperial designs and western reproductions. This article is a call

for a functional yet aesthetic design in the service of history, ecology, and the people.

After already struggling with the foreign Manchu rule and failed reforms at the turn of the last century, China's lack of international standing was exemplified in 1919 at the Versailles peace conference, when concessions were lost to western countries. Students took to the streets on May 4th, 1919 to protest the decline of their nation. At the same time, in an attempt to combat China's general backwardness, a cultural revolution took place, which, although spearheaded by China's leftist intellectuals, reached every layer of society. It was this movement, the New Cultural Movement (1917–1937) that "called to arms" all those who were willing to help transform China into a stronger nation. Lu Xun (1881–1936), the most famous intellectual writer of the period, called on the nation to rise out of the "iron house" of complacency into cultivating a critical consciousness that would, through democracy, science, and social equality, lead to progress in China. This iconoclastic "obsession with China" (C.T. Hsia) was a hallmark of May 4th writing. The most important tool to generate the socio-political changes, was the change in literature from classical Chinese to the vernacular. It was Lu Xun who wrote the first modern short story in the vernacular, and his indictment of stifling Confucian traditions quickly became the prototype of the May 4th intellectual agenda. Yet, in spite of the seemingly hopeless state of the Chinese national character, his story, *A Madman's Diary*, ended on a hopeful call to at least "save the children".

Since the 1980s, another paradigm shift has taken place, at least in urban China, from modernity to post-modernity. But because of the rapid and often chaotic socio-political transformations since

then, the country is facing two major crises that cannot be overlooked: the crisis of national cultural identity again, and of the human–land relationship.

Traditionally, Chinese identity was based on the feudalistic social and political order of the dynasties. In fact, when we look at the architectural hallmarks of China even now, most items listed are artifacts of the imperial ages. While past achievements are not rebuffed, it is not necessary to ask if this style still represents national identity in China today. In addition, China now battles issues of globalization, rampant materialism, post-modernity, and rapid urbanization. This identity crisis is particularly obvious in the area of urban design. When a French designer puts his masterpiece (the Grand Opera House) into the center of China's capital to realize his own dream, or when a majestic but "dysfunctional" Central TV Tower is built only for the "power to bewitch" (Daniel Burnham), designers must ask how ephemeral such endeavors are, or if they don't simply impede the May 4th path to democracy, science, and progress. Torn between its imperial past and today's westernization, it raises questions about Chinese identity today.

If the landscape is a symbol and expression of cultural identification, what constitutes the crisis of environmental collectivity? One hundred years ago, the relationship between the people and the land was primarily one of survival. But in China today, an ecological crisis is added to the national identity crisis. The disregard for the environment has given rise to an unbridled rape of nature, to the destruction of biotopes, of the ecological equilibrium, and to an exhaustion of the "yellow earth", all in the name of urbanization and modernization, and often even under the tutelage of designers and planners.

Urbanization and urban sprawl have altered the entire Chinese landscape, and in many cases have turned fertile land into central business districts that are void of atmosphere and polluted. The human–land crisis in China is unprecedented in its destruction of fields, natural forests, wetlands, and prairies, and will lead to an increased ecological imbalance that threatens everyone's anthroposphere (Lebensraum).

Just as during the May 4th Movement, the literary vernacular was the language of a cultural revolution that embraced the entire citizenship of the nation, and just as Dr Hu Shih (1891–1962) argued that a dead language cannot create a living literature, a landscape cannot be supported that is based on relics and empty crossbreeds, that calls forth the souls of the dead, or is a mere reproduction of western design. While each has its place and time, China's land needs a vernacular-style landscape and architecture design.

Why is landscape architecture and architecture in China lagging behind in the "modern project"? First, the May 4th Movement was too short-lived to completely obliterate the old spirit of feudalism; second, many excellent designers and architects suffered under the often-chaotic political circumstances of the ensuing 50 years, and had no opportunity to develop professionally; third, against the backdrop of westernization and modernization in the 1980s, two schools of thought contended that are equally antagonistic toward a true modernization of design with Chinese characteristics: the first school holds western influences in high esteem and misinterprets western design (or simply western form) as the only modern design; the other simply wants to recapture the imperial style of traditional Chinese architecture.

A vernacular style of cities and landscapes in China neither simply imitates western-style design nor the imperial Chinese tradition but is based on the May 4th spirit of democracy, science and the community. Although there are many modernist buildings in our cities, they do not capture the essence and the spirit of a modern Chinese architecture. Although China's imperial gardens, for example, are a worthy historical legacy, they are also a specter haunting landscape architects today. Now that we have the tools and the freedom to practice modern design, it is time to establish the May 4th vernacular project in landscape architecture. Such a design is useful for a broad citizenship, quotidian, functional, and aesthetic, conceived with a landscape ethic that combines the originality of a place with a sound ecological approach. To be innovative and thoughtful in landscape design is what all children deserve.

What then does a vernacular landscape design look like? One prize-winning example is the Zhongshan Shipyard Park in Zhongshan City, Guangdong, China. Built on the site of a deserted dockyard, this park is a beacon of five decades of socialist history. For those who have lived and worked there during those times, it still stirs nostalgic feelings reminiscent of a very distinct work ethic, and in others it evokes curiosity and imagination. In a country like China, in particular, many places have monuments that recall history, but this park is unique in that it combines, in its metamorphosis into a modern park, structural changes that allow for both education and leisure. Unlike the traditional Lingnan gardens of this area with their pavilions and artificial ponds, this park is integrated into the modern infrastructure of the town and the area. Reused railroad embankments, water systems, workshops, machine houses, and

other heavy machinery and equipment remain as witnesses of its industrial past. In addition to preserving the essence of this blue-collar past, some of the original landscape and horticulture of the place have been restored, Located within the Pearl River Delta, it is one of the richest agricultural areas with an immensely luscious flower and grass culture. In addition, it seemed appropriate to use valuable design approaches of non-geometric garden designs, and, more importantly, the modern approaches of environmentalism, ecological restoration, and so-called 'new urbanization', of which the Ruhr valley parks in Germany are a paramount example. Yet, in comparison with the spectacular industrial structures one can see in Ruhr and the Gas Station Project in Seattle, USA, the Old Zhongshan Shipyard is not significant in terms of its industrial structures. It therefore needs more new designs in order to make the site enjoyable. The outcome is what we call a "chaotic" economy: not a formally defined beauty or a geometrical design, not a rusty reserve of industrial structures, but rather cobweb structures, beeline footpaths, railroad walking trails, the simple but elegant beauty of wild grasses, the simple but meaningful new design of a red box. The goals of this design are numerous: to preserve its specific local history, to restore some of the original landscape and its eco-system, to reuse the location for education and leisure, and to tell the story of the memorable past and of the common people. The Zhongshan Shipyard Park is a historical landmark in progress, a patch of common wild grass beauty, and a signpost of ongoing change.

1.4 A Force of Nature

China's Top Landscape Architect is on a Quest to Bring Unexpected Beauty to the Country's Boomtowns

Susan Jakes, Time Asia Magazine

In 1999, city officials in Zhongshan decided to tear down a shipyard and replace it with a park. The city, situated across the mouth of the Pearl River from Hong Kong, has a tradition of putting its wealth to good civic use. Its streets are tidy and lined with flowerbeds and well-maintained trees, and its council has received many awards from both Beijing and the United Nations for its tidy appearance. But these shiny credentials presented a dilemma for local leaders, as their political promotion would depend in part on outdoing their predecessors, and Zhongshan didn't leave much room for improvement. So when the Yuezhong shipworks went bankrupt, it wasn't long before plans emerged to remove the eyesore and make progress.

Landscape architect Yu Kongjian attended from Beijing to give the project some impetus, and as is often the case, his first move was to throw a wrench into the plans. Zhongshan didn't need more flowers, Yu told the city officials; it didn't need fountains, ornate wrought-iron fences, or hedges shaped like animals. Instead of bulldozing the shipyard, he proposed, they could put it to new use. A gantry crane would make an interesting gate, a crumbling water tower could become the base of a lighted beacon. Instead of grass, the city should grow weeds. Zhongshan's leaders found the plan unsettling. "We wanted something distinctive, but this made us nervous", says He Shaoyang, then head of the city's planning commission. "It wasn't like a Chinese garden with a rock here and a tree there". But, in time, the ecological soundness and low cost of Yu's ideas won them over. "After all," says He, "Zhongshan has a lot of parks. They shouldn't all have to look the same".

That's an unusual attitude in today's China. The nation is in the phase of the fastest urban growth in human history. In recent years the country has built an average of 2 billion square meters of floor space annually, half the world's yearly total, and has plans to add another 20–30 billion by 2020. In theory, this should offer limitless opportunities for innovative urban planning. But as China's cities have grown larger, they have only become more uniform, so that each now seems to boast a skyscraping government office, roads scaled like highways and a vast Tiananmen-like square. This alikeness results largely from a dearth of professional designers and from the fact that breakneck growth leaves scant time for subtlety. But it also reflects a value system in which city infrastructure is conceived in symbolic rather than practical terms and where extravagance is the accepted symbol for modernity.

Yu, a professor of landscape architecture at Peking University, argues that China's current approach to urban development, with its emphasis on size and status over originality, is as environmentally reckless as it is visually dull. With farmland and forests disappearing and water running out, Yu says, cities can't afford to be so wasteful: "China needs a dramatic shift. We've misunderstood what it means to be developed. We need to develop a new system, a new vernacular, to express the changing relationship between land and people". When Yu, now 42, returned home in 1997 with a doctorate in design from Harvard and a teaching appointment at Peking University's Architecture Center, landscape design wasn't even an officially recognized profession. The country had a long tradition of private gardens cultivated by gentry, and more recently austere Stalinist-style parks designed to project state authority. But he felt the country needed more. "Landscape architects can't just be garden artists", says Yu. So, in 1998, he founded Turenscape, China's first private landscape design firm, and set about finding places like Zhongshan where officials were willing to try something different.

Turen is an odd name for a Chinese company. *Ren* means person, but *tu* is more complicated. Literally the word translates as "earth" or "soil", but it's often used as a slur, a put-down for anything that is backward or unsophisticated the manners of a migrant worker, bad teeth, and cloth shoes. When Yu's colleagues answer the phone, "Turen", it sounds like they're calling themselves bumpkins. Yu himself remembers being called *tu* when he arrived in Beijing from a rice farm in Zhejiang to enroll at the Beijing University of Forestry in 1980. He was 17, could barely speak Mandarin and was awestruck by the straightness of the city's poplar-lined roads. This "farmerist outlook", as Yu describes his own first impressions of Beijing, is the reason Chinese cities look the way they do: "We're a country of farmers. When we make it to the city we want to feel as far away from the land as possible. We hate weeds. We want to look up at tall buildings. We shun nature". To be truly urban, Yu says, China needs a new attitude toward *tu*.

When Premier Wen Jiabao opened the annual National People's Congress with a speech about building a "new socialist countryside", Yu headed for the town of Changgou, in a rural district of Beijing, "to try to save some trees". Friends in the district government had phoned with news that Changgou had announced it would bulldoze several of its constituent villages and bring in 5000 laborers to create an enormous man-made lake as part of a program to attract real estate investment and tourism. They'd recommended that local leaders give Yu an audience and consider hiring him. "It sounds like the Great Leap Forward", Mao's disastrous campaign to boost economic productivity in the 1950s, Yu had said, as he sped toward Changgou in a van full of landscape designers. "But maybe I can stop them".

A group of local leaders took Yu on a tour of their project. Chalk lines marking the lake's proposed shores ran through villages and along roads. Yu leapt out of the car to take photos of a pair of bulldozers that looked tiny against the vast swath of empty land where they were mounding up dirt. Bounding past the officials, he turned his camera on a bird's nest high up in a poplar next to the mineral spring supposed to supply the lake. "He even takes pictures of that", marveled one official when Yu was out of earshot. Driving through town Yu passed a cluster of empty villas, waiting for the lakeside they'd overlook. Nearby, on a fenced-off piece of grass grazed an elephant and a giraffe, both made of plaster.

Back at the town office, the officials presented their plan. They played a video presentation that showed pictures of large lakes in other places. Changgou's lake would be the center of a new resort, they told Yu. They would have windsurfing, golf and maybe skiing. The video presentation included a montage of flowers opening in time-lapse followed by pictures of ripe fruit and beachside cottages. "This is our concept", one official told Yu, as the screen filled with hot-air balloons.

When it was Yu's turn to speak, he smiled. "I think you have a very good idea", he said quietly. "But I don't think your lake needs to be quite so big. What you have here is very rare. You're one of the only places in North China with spring water. If you use it up to make a giant lake, no one will come here. Right now I'm worried you're going to spend a lot of money, but lose value. Other places have lakes. Why not do something different? You could be a model of innovation".

Yu showed some slides of his work. "Wild grass", he said, pausing for emphasis. "It can be beautiful. It's very modern". Before long someone brought him a box of children's markers and a map, and he went to work sketching in islands of existing rice paddies within the planned lake's neat, rectangular perimeter. The official in charge of the project (who asked not to be named) winced. "I have plenty of paddies in this town", he told Yu. "If people want to look at them, they can go somewhere else. I don't need paddies in my lake".

The power of Yu's designs is the succinctness with which they communicate his ideas. His parks pair bushy tufts of native plants (which don't need to be watered or trimmed) with angular paths and minimalist sculptures in brightly colored metal. The contrast between these rustic and futuristic elements is intended to attract people to the natural landscape, while changing it as little a possible. Yu studies the sites of his projects intensively before he starts planning and tries to work with what's already there's an approach he calls "anti-planning".

In Shenyang, when an architecture school moved to the suburbs, Yu designed its campus to incorporate the rice paddies of the farms it had displaced. The rice became both a decorative element and a kind of literal food for thought and reminder that landscaping needn't be expensive and that even agriculture can look modern. In Taizhou, Yu un-channeled a local river, removing cement barriers and letting it flood into a wetland through which he snaked bicycle paths, docks and terraces. In Zhongshan, Yu's shipyard park, which like the campus was honored by the American Society of Landscape Architects, has quickly become a local landmark. On a recent weekday afternoon, the park was full. Toddlers climbed happily over pebbled railroad tracks, men played chess on a platform surrounded by tall reeds, a bride posed for a portrait amid some (deliberately) un-raked leaves, and two vanloads of officials on a study tour listened to a guide talk about environmental protection.

Despite his success as a designer, Yu sees himself primarily as an educator. In 2003 he founded his personally funded China's first graduate program in landscape architecture (at Peking University) and he serves as its dean. He writes prolifically and, again at his own expense, has mailed copies of his book, *The Road to Urban Landscape: A Discussion with Mayors*, to some 3000 city

Figure 35 Shenyang Architectural University campus features a rice paddy (Photo: Cao Yang)

Figure 36 The Zhongshan Shipyard Park. (Photo: Li, J.K.)

36

officials. The book is a direct but gently mocking assault on monumentalism: its illustrations show absurdly massive plazas and people squatting on low fences designed to keep them off mosaics of hedges that can only be appreciated from the sky. Recently, Yu's ideas have gained new traction in high places. Environmental sustainability, green growth and resource conservation were major themes of last month's meeting of the National People's Congress. And Yu has been approved to help Shanghai rehabilitate a decrepit industrial stretch of its main river for its 2010 World Expo and to create a corridor of parkland along 1700 meters of the Grand Canal.

But it's the smaller victories that seem to excite him the most. The day after his visit, Changgou's leaders called to say they'd accept his plan. "I'm putting in islands and bike paths", says Yu. "The rice paddies are staying. They'll be beautiful".

Reprinted with permission from *Time Asia Magazine*, April 10, 2006, Vol. 167, No. 14

Figure 37 In Taizhou, Yu stop the process of channelization and un-channeled a local river, removing cement barriers and letting it flood into a wetland through which he snaked bicycle paths, docks and terraces;
Lower right of the photo: the former channelized river side;
Left: the ecologically recovered section (the Yongning River Park) at the former channelized riverside at the left side;
Upper right: un-channeled river bank but not accessible to people. (Photo: Cao, Y.)

1.5 Questions and Answers about Landscape Architecture

The International Federation of Landscape Architects' Eastern Region (IFLAer) Conference was held in Sydney in May 2006. National and international speakers addressed the pivotal role of time and change in the practice of the built environment professions and the effects on contemporary society and the landscape. Kongjian Yu, dean and professor of the Graduate School of Landscape Architecture at Peking University answers some questions about the practice of landscape architecture and the state of the profession.

Kongjian Yu, ASLA

Dean and Professor, The Graduate School of Landscape Architecture, Peking University and President, Turenscape, Beijing, China

1 What places, projects, or people have had the greatest influence on your professional career?

My childhood experiences of growing up in a small, traditional Chinese village greatly influenced my understanding of landscape and landscape architecture. It was a simple agricultural community, but for me it is the landscape where nature, humans and the spirit come together. I spent a lot of time along a stream with willow trees and diverse shrubs growing alongside it that protected the fields from being eroded. While my water buffalo enjoyed the lush grasses at the water's edge I enjoyed catching fish. This became the model stream for my design.

The experience of fieldwork and irrigation, walking across the rice paddies and through the patterned fields resulting from the rotation of crops, influenced my understanding about grading, scale, color, and pattern (*Figures 38–42*).

The settlement itself is a model for my thinking about "people's place": the central square where the villagers got together, the corner space where a mill was located, the place under the aged camphor tree where my grandfather told stories, and the stone bridge with the shrines for the Earth Spirits, these places are all about useful and meaningful landscapes.

2 Identify your favorite public space or project (not one on which you've worked) and explain why.

Two sets of public projects dramatically changed my understanding about landscape projects and the criteria for a good landscape works.

The first set is the ancient waterworks of Li Qu (Magic Trench) and Dujiangyan Weir in China, both built more than 2000 years ago and still functioning today for multiple purposes. They

Figure 38 The rice paddies and grave yard of the author's home village. (Photo: Yu, K.J.)

Figures 39–41 Inspired by the experience of rice paddies, the Shengyang Architectural School Campus was designed by the author to create a productive and affordable landscape while fulfilling the needs for new functions at the same time. (Photo: Yu, K.J. and Cao. Y)

demonstrate how humankind, by using minimum technology, can harness even the most fearful of natural forces for human needs without sacrificing nature's interests. The skill of negotiation and mutual understanding between natural and cultural forces make these projects sustainable, useful, beautiful, and inspiring.

The other set is Richard Haag's Gasworks Park in Seattle, Washington and Peter Latz's Duisburg North Landscape Park in Germany. They show how a functional but "ugly" landscape that was considered useless can become "beautiful" again.

These two pioneer works that protected and reused industrial sites dramatically changed the values and ethics about our cultural heritage.

We value landscapes that must be useful now, or that used to be useful, and it is these landscapes that give me a lot of inspiration (*Figures 43–50*).

3 Nominate a space or project (either one you've worked on or would like to discuss) that has demonstrated positive environmental outcomes and explain how.

I was involved in designing the Shengyang Architectural University Campus, Shengyang City, China, which is an example demonstrating how landscape architects can address big issues that result in positive environmental outcomes.

The overwhelming urbanization process in China is inevitably encroaching upon a great amount of arable land. With a population of 1.3 billion people and limited arable land resources, food production and sustainable land use are the biggest issues in China, which the profession of landscape architecture should address.

This campus design uses rice paddies and other native crops to keep the land as productive as it was while fulfilling the need for new functions at the same time. It is designed to raise the awareness of the land and farming among the young generation leaving the countryside to become city dwellers. This project also demonstrates that the inexpensive and productive agricultural landscape can become, through

39

careful design and management, a beautiful and usable space as well (*Figures 38,40,41*).

4 Explain your perspective on how successful the profession has been in dealing with the most pressing environmental concerns.

Half a century ago, Hideo Sasaki commented that "the profession of landscape architecture stands at a critical fork in the road. One fork leads to a significant field of endeavor contributing to the betterment of human environment, while the other points to a subordinate field of superficial embellishment". Unfortunately, except for some rare cases, landscape architecture in the past decade has become more "a subordinate field of superficial embellishment". We could have taken a more important role in the most pressing environmental issues such as flood control and water management, the protection of biodiversity, cultural heritage protection, urbanization, and land resources management. One of the major reasons is that landscape architecture as a profession is still associated in the public perception and in university textbooks, with the ancient tradition of gardening. The rich heritage and literature about landscape gardening and garden art did not help landscape architecture to emerge as a modern discipline. It is about time to declare that modern landscape architecture does not stem from the art of landscape gardening, but

40

that landscape architecture (planning and design) is rooted more in our ancestor's struggle with such big issues as flood management, making places for settlements, and cultivating the land, than in pleasure-making and gardening.

5 Aims and wishes for the future of the profession. What do you think are the main challenges and opportunities for landscape architects in the next few decades?

Urbanization, globalization, and the spread of materialism have positioned landscape architecture to critically address three major challenges in the coming decades.

The first is the survival of humanity on earth. More than ever, large parts of the population are exposed to disastrous natural forces, pollution, and a shortage of resources, as the tsunami in Asia, Hurricane Katrina in New Orleans, and numerous floods each year all over the world have demonstrated. Two thirds of the 662 Chinese cities are in shortage of water, and all rivers in the urban and suburban areas are polluted. Taking land as a medium, landscape architecture is given the great opportunities within this crucial period of time to find ways of rebuilding a harmonious relationship between the land and people.

The second is about cultural identity. The strength of landscape architecture in dealing with this issue lies in its intrinsic association with the natural systems and in its roots of agricultural tradition. Urbanization and globalization processes are so fast and overwhelming, that a "negative approach" should be taken against the conventional development planning, that is, landscape architects and planners should lead the way to identify and design an ecological infrastructure that is critical in safeguarding the ecological processes and cultural heritages, before the stage of land-use planning.

The third is the protection and rebuilding of our spiritual homeland. The trend of materialism has been taking over the world and also China. The land, which used to be inhabited by various spirits that made the landscape meaningful and poetic, is becoming commercialized. Gradually, we lose our spiritual connections to our land to superficial, exchangeable international images of the world beyond the earthly one, which landscape architecture is positioned to protect and rebuild.

"Landscape architecture is the profession of the future", to quote IFLA president Martha Fajardo (2005), and the future's profession lies in its unique position to deal with the land as a medium, where the natural, cultural, and the spiritual processes interact, and where all these processes can be integrated harmoniously. But this future will be ours only if we are prepared.

Reprinted from: *Landscape Australia*, No.109, February 2006, pp.46–48

Figure 42 The wetland park in the Life Science Park, Beijing, China, designed by the author and was inspired by the experience of rice paddies. (Photo:Yu, K.J.)

Figure 43 The inspiring Lin Qu water works built more than 2000 years ago still functions today. (Photo: Yu, K.J.)

Figures 44,45 An urban water feature designed by the author and inspired by the ancient Chinese water works. (Photo: Yu, K.J., and Cao. Y.)

46

Figures 46–50 The Zhongshan Shipyard Park, Guangdong, China, features industrial heritage. It was designed by the author and partly inspired by the pioneering works of industrial site protection in Germany and the USA. (Photo: Yu, K.J., and Cao. Y.)

1.6 Urban Frenzy

Beijing Today *meets a man who thinks the first step in China's city planning education should be an apology from architect Rem Koolhaas.*

Gareth George, Beijing Today

51

Figure 51 Famous Western architects Koolhaas, Andreu have to make a decision. They must know that a building is inappropriate for China, but they also must come up with the most outrageous design or they won't win the contract. So they are asked to choose between money and fame or a responsible attitude.
"We can't mimic others, because we have a different climate and lifestyle to New York or Europe. We have a different culture and should express it. Even a different sense of color." (Courtesy OMA)

The office is like a jungle, with spidery plants in plump urns reaching almost to the ceiling. A medal from the Chinese Academy of Fine Arts rests beside a spectrum of magic markers. Dry leaves have fallen onto the black wood desk littered with wooden mushrooms and padded cushions. Almost hidden amongst the clutter, Professor Kongjian Yu fears for his country. He places his teacup precariously between stacks of printed paper and a couple of laptop computers and talks about today as the biggest turning point in Chinese history since May 4th, 1919. Yu believes that, once again, China is experiencing a crisis of national cultural identity. This time, the issue is the relationship between the people and their homeland.

Nowadays, when Yu speaks, people listen. He received his doctorate from Harvard's Graduate School of Design in 1995, and spent two years practicing in Los Angeles with the SWA Group before returning to China. As well as founding the Graduate School of Landscape Architecture at Peking University, Yu is also founder and President of Turenscape, the largest landscape and urban design company in China. And he finds much about Beijing's landscape to trouble him.

Professor Yu believes that Beijing is in the process of a "beautiful city" movement, a term first used to describe The Chicago Exhibition of 1893, and that Beijing's urbanization mirrors events in North America a century ago. Like China today, the US became a rich nation "overnight", and wanted to demonstrate this to the world. "They bought things from Europe, imported art, exported exhibitions to show off their wealth. And they looked at what they had seen as powerful—the great imperial European cities—and they mimicked them".

Today, China wants to show the world its strength, its power. "Here landscape, architecture and the urban environment become the tools to show off—like a peacock. When you dress up, you try to show off your identity, your values, your aesthetic taste".

But America woke up. Yu explains that America finally realized that the beautiful city movement was costing huge sums while creating a few pretty buildings and a lot of social problems. Theorists began to talk of a "vernacular landscape" one that would reflect the true native identity. But this was almost 80 years after the initial damage was done. And the process of fixing the damage is one that continues even today. Yu feels that China is repeating the same mistakes and failing to learn the lessons of the past. "The identity of today's Chinese is not yet found", he adds.

Yu sees three distinct identities struggling for space in Beijing today. The first is the classical European style, which the Americans also copied. This romantic style comes mainly from France, Italy, and England. "The style of Kings: imperial, foreboding and outdated", he says. The second is the "modern style". China as a rapidly modernizing country, naturally wants to reflect this. But Yu believes this modern fixation has led China in the wrong direction too. "We look to what we think is modern: New York; the big American cities. And that is modern, but it's modern imperialism. The image of a modern capitalist society, with palaces for the capitalist emperors. It reflects America, but not China. Koolhaas' CCTV building falls into this category, or at least, it's a Chinese feudalist emperor in modern dress".

Third, as China becomes a great nation on a global scale, many look to reimpose the grandeur of the past. "We have 5000 years of history. Many want to rebuild the imperial image of China. That's why so many buildings feature marble and dragons. This has happened before with ancient nations that have seen a city beautiful movement—Italy and Germany in the 1930s tried to recapture old glories for a new age". But none of these three schools represent what Yu sees as "the true identity of the modern Chinese".

The problem with the city beautiful movement is that it is interested in cosmetic form over function; great buildings at the expense of a utilitarian city.

In his keynote speech to the Beijing Architecture Biennale, Professor Alexander Garvin of Yale University and author of *The American City: What Works, What Doesn't*, stated that China is far from the first nation to fall into this trap. "When it comes to great city building, the solution is planning. The reason successes are so often overlooked is because when a problem is solved it's forgotten", he says. Good planning, he adds, is the key ingredient to a city's "safety, utility, and quality of life".

Most major nations have experienced planning disasters. And now they're spending big to correct them. But China comes to the table with a blank slate, and yet while Europe and even the US are looking to more efficient forms of public transport to improve quality of life and limit pollution, China is embracing the car. "Twenty years ago we had a very green transport system, with excellent cycle paths. Now we combat traffic problems by building wider roads, so we have not one lane jams, but four or five lane ones", says Yu.

Fifty years ago, America and Europe were channeling their rivers. Now they are spending millions to dig them back up, while China begins to channel hers. "There are no natural rivers in Beijing now, while the west is finding that natural rivers, far from being a waste of space, can contribute to the success of local business, and encourage tourism. This is the ecological approach". Yu talks about the "Big Dig Project" in Boston for which he won the urban design competition, the China Town Park Design, with a local design firm in 2002. "It was simple, we dug down and put part of the highway underground, leaving the open air streets for public transport, cyclists and pedestrians. For daily use. This kind of project is worth our attention".

Rather than lay the blame with specific individuals, Professor Yu believes that the system has evolved in a way that makes coherent planning difficult. "Right now half of China's richest people make their money from the land. The process of urbanization, where people can draw a line and say, 'This land is developable, and therefore saleable' means that a lot of people are becoming hugely wealthy overnight. So these people get this huge profit, become rich and powerful, then they don't know how to spend it. So each of them wants to build the highest, most expensive building. A luxury plaza, a central street just to have a beautiful thing without considering its function. Or how the city will work around it".

Chinese cities operate a zoning system, similar to that of the old USSR and the US. And the US has experienced the problems that China is now seeing. Land is sold according to a plan, within defined "lines". One area will be sold as a real estate zone, the next a commercial zone. So the city emerges piece by piece, with little consideration for the organic unit. The potential is for a city that favors the car over green transport and thus becomes polluted. And a city that segregates rich and poor areas into zones that may be separated by just a retail area.

Elsewhere in the world, this has led to ugly, forgotten districts that promote only poverty and social unrest. "China needs an intellectual movement to go forward", says Yu. "We need to make the decision process more scientific and more democratic".

Yu doesn't believe that the city authorities are yet receiving adequate advice, from their own people or from the foreign architects they bring in. "The people with power have an idea of what they want: a grand building, a unique symbol. This might not be the best thing for the city, but then the famous western architects—Koolhaas, Andreu—have to make a decision. They must know that a building is inappropriate for China, but they also must come up with the most outrageous design or they won't win the contract. So they are asked to choose money and fame or a responsible attitude".

"At this stage what China really needs is education". Yu says, "We don't have a modern identity. We need to understand what's good and bad, what's imperialistic and what's capitalist. What is for the upstart nation and what is for the people. We need to know the difference between formal modernism and spiritual modernism. The Western architects should be coming here as teachers, not just to take the money ... especially the big ones, like Koolhaas. They should be setting an example of what is suitable for this nation".

To this effect, Yu has presented ideas to more than 600 mayors as part of this education. But with the big contracts still going to companies from overseas, the tide has not yet turned. Work began in October (2004) on the new CCTV building designed by Rem Koolhaas and Yu uses this to illustrate all that he feels is wrong with the city beautiful movement. "It's formally modern, but spiritually imperialistic ... a very capitalist building. A more functional building could have been built for a tenth of the cost, and with billions here in China without access to formal schooling this is against democracy and the scientific way. Instead of using the most simple method to solve a problem, the CCTV building is a misuse of technology to show off".

Professor Yu believes that the first step in China's education should be an apology from Koolhaas. "Of course, Koolhaas was asked to build this, and I don't want to criticize his talent, if he hadn't taken the contract, maybe some worse architect would have. But when Einstein developed nuclear power, he sent out a message when he admitted his regret. I would like to see Koolhaas set this example to other architects and planners in China and admit the building is unsuitable for Beijing".

With education, Yu believes that China will come to see its own path. "We can't mimic others, because we have a different climate and lifestyle to New York or Europe. We have a different culture and should express it. Even a different sense of color. Tomorrow, we will have the self-confidence to express ourselves. Hopefully before the destruction of the unique identity of this place and our people".

And people are starting to listen. Yu has received invitations from many real estate developers and city governments to design projects all over the country, and although his single-minded nature has meant that these projects have not always been 100 percent successful, it also means he won't ever give up.

Gareth George has been a freelance feature writer in Beijing since 2004. He is also features editor for English language newspaper *Beijing Today*.

Reprinted with permission from *Beijing Today*, December 17, 2004

1.7 Internationality and Cultural Identity

The Search For a Contemporary Design Idiom in China

Antje Stokman and Stefanie Ruff

Garden design has a long tradition in China. Modern landscape architecture is still searching to develop its own style between traditional examples and international monotony. Projects by Turenscape demonstrate elements of a contemporary yet autonomous language of design.

China is known for the age-old art of planning gardens that look like three-dimensional paintings that are symbols of harmony between nature and man. China, the fourth-largest country on earth, is also known for a large variety of spectacular cultural landscapes. These have evolved over centuries of adapting ways land is transformed in various natural conditions and numerous climatic zones. Extensive knowledge of nature's cycles and integrating humans into these cycles has flowed into the design of the landscape. Historians also agree that by continually clearing, terracing, turning the soil, planting and irrigating, the Chinese have influenced their environment in a more long-lasting way than any other nation.

Due to current trends in city development, the construction industry is booming. Skyscrapers, fashionable residential districts, software technology parks and shopping centers are springing up everywhere—the landscape is being developed at a rate never experienced before, causing an increasingly damaging impact on the environment. Everything seems possible, and at a dizzying rate. Environmental and recreational consciousness is increasing along with rising levels of income, prosperity and education. The need for an enduring form of organization and design of urban spaces is growing steadily. What options exist for the profession of landscape architecture in China, in light of its historic roots and current trends in city development? And how are these options reflected in the current position and trends in developing contemporary Chinese landscape architecture?

To many foreigners visiting China, the diversity of cultural landscapes appears like a large garden with a mosaic of dams, terraces and fields. Differing greatly from the Egyptians, who lived in inhospitable deserts and planned their gardens

52

53

on the desert borders in the same rational way as their fruit orchards or wheat fields, the Chinese never copied their cultural landscapes in their gardens. In traditional Chinese garden design, rather than being artificially stylized or formal geometric compositions, the gardens were a miniature concentration of natural landscape images created by a compression of familiar landscape scenarios. The garden, "heaven and earth in one vessel", according to a quotation from a scholar from the Tang Dynasty (618–907), represents the universe, with its many landscape elements such as brooks, hills, springs, ponds, islands, pavilions, plants and cliffs.

Today many Chinese designs are still characterized by the placement of too many elements in a limited space, and of not only imitating nature, but also creating miniature copies of Chinese and international models. Whereas the European tradition of lawns is associated with nature's freshness and brightness from the tradition of the shepherd, the Chinese associate their grass with the wilderness that threatens their civilization. As recently as 1920, a Chinese traveler described the expansive lawns in European parks as good for cows, but not suitable for the human intellect. Today, however, lawns are symbols of internationalism and luxury. Native plants and natural ecosystem development are still considered uncivilized. Until now, designs which use ornamental, strongly decorative and axial language, are dominating. The designs lack a relationship to the context. Set pieces identifiable as being traditionally Chinese, such as pagoda forms, symbolic stone formations and plant varieties, paired with European Baroque hedges and sculptural elements, and expensive, modern materials, create a colorful mixture of styles. The style mixture is a symbol of a commerce- and progress-

oriented culture. This condition is caused by client preconceptions and their strong need to have these represented; the taste of the fast-growing Chinese middle and upper classes, and their desire to display their newly acquired wealth in a respective living environment; and also the different educational backgrounds of the architects involved.

Whereas garden architecture on a small scale has been a tradition in China for centuries, landscape architecture has only existed as an independent planning discipline for the last 20 years. The field of landscape architecture takes on particular significance in light of current urban expansion and environmental problems; significant not only in enhancing the landscape in cities, but also in developing ideas to solve problems related to ecology, infrastructure and use. Solutions can hardly be gathered from limited traditional understanding of the field, using the restricted garden design model, or be borrowed from foreign examples. How can a landscape architect in China fulfill the needs and aspirations of modern man to become international, and also satisfy local and regional requirements?

Most frequently it is young offices, established by architects who have often studied internationally, that have new answers in developing a modern understanding in the field. They are trying to provide new stimulus to the field and to question current trends in the practice. One representative of the young Chinese landscape architects is Kongjian Yu. He grew up in a small village in the Zhejiang province, characterized by its traditional rural use of open spaces. He studied garden planning at the Peking Forestry University, the largest and oldest landscape architecture school in China (founded in 1952). Later he earned his doctorate at Harvard. After returning to China in 1998, he established

Turenscape in Beijing. The office, with a staff of approximately 200, is the largest private landscape architecture firm in China today.

Kongjian Yu has described today's China as having an identity crisis as well as an ecological crisis. He is striving to create an appropriately modern and Chinese identity in his writings, planning and design projects, and in the new landscape architecture program he established at the Peking University. While doing so, he seeks a strong relationship to the genius loci: a design approach that stems from a particular place, the context of its natural and cultural landscape, and the associated local traditions of the people. In formulating his designs he is creating a new consciousness for the beauty of the Chinese cultural landscape and indigenous vegetation— a completely new concept for China.

In designing the campus for Shenyang University, Turenscape captures the original structure of the agricultural landscape by using the path as divisions between the rice field parcels. The configuration of the design is rectilinear; its motif is unusual for a university campus—that of a productive cultural landscape whose products are harvested and sold as souvenirs. The site is broken into spaces varying in size, divided by a strong framework of diagonally arranged rows of single trees and tree groves, as well as a rectilinear axis of walkways. The geometry of the park is taken from the rational order of the surrounding agricultural fields, and the diagonal orientation of the parcels. The design combines the artificiality of a French Baroque garden with cultural and wild vegetation plantings in an exemplary, ornamented grid—an unusual learning environment for the architecture students.

Zhongguancun Life Science Park in Peking is a

project that uses a central park area as a wetland system. A network of walkways leads one through a mosaic of different native aquatic plants and reeds. Paths on different levels linked by steps make various connections possible across areas with varying water levels.

In the Yongning River Park in Taizhou, an area transformed into a native reed and grass landscape was once part of the artificial embankment of the river. Additional flood plains were returned to the river through this change and assisted in water purification of the natural wetlands. The park design includes an organically shaped wetland system at the same level as the river. The area of the wetlands is contrasted by square bastions planted with a grid of Chinese redwoods (Metasequoia glyptostroboides) distributed along the linear-shaped wetland. The Chinese redwood is common along riparian landscapes in southern China. Circulation within the park is provided by an axial grid of paths, partly comprised of elevated bridges and walkways. An unusual feature of the park is the scattered colorful square boxes that serve as special areas for the visitors.

In the Turenscape projects, new issues for China are apparent. These concern ecological and dynamic processes of nature, such as changing water levels, seasons, ecosystem development, vegetation, and harvests. These considerations, plus the design philosophy of using native wild and cultural vegetation, retaining and utilizing historical structures and minimizing the design language, enable Turenscape to create new ideas for combining Chinese cultural identity with international examples.

55

The Landscape Master Plan
for Life Science Park, Beijing

Storm water co... land

Storm water collection(we...

The area presented in detail

Recycled sewage water goes to wet l...

Recycled sewage water goes to wet land

Recycled sewage water goes to wet land

56

57

Projects:

Shenyang Architectural Campus, Shenyang City
(Figures 52–55)

Client: Shenyang Architectural University

Landscape Architects: Turenscape

Realization: 2002–2003

Size: 80 hectares

Photos: Yu, K.J.

Zhongguancun Life Science Park, Beijing
(Figures 56–59)

Client: Peking Zhongguancun Life Science Park
Development Co., Ltd.

Landscape Architects: Turenscape

Realization: 2001–2002

Size: 10 Hectares

Photos: Yu, K.J., and Cao, Y.

Yongning River Park, Taizhou City *(Figures 60–63)*

Client: The Government of Huangyan District,
Taizhou City

Landscape Architect: Turenscape

Realization: 2002–2004

Size: 21.3 hectares

Photos: Yu, K.J.

Antje Stokman, born in 1973, studied landscape architecture at the University of Hanover and Edinburgh College of Art. After graduation she worked as a research and teaching assistant in the University of Hanover from 2000–2001 and in "Rainer Schmidt Landschaftsarchitekten" from 2001–2004. Since 2004 she has undertaken freelance work as well as research and teaching in the University of Hanover, guest lecturer at TU Hamburg Harburg in Germany and Peking University, and Tongji University Shanghai, China.

Stefanie Ruff, born in 1976, trained as a gardener and studied landscape architecture at TFH Berlin. During her studies she gained work experience in different landscape offices in Berlin and Australia, and since 2004 she has undertaken freelance work for different landscape architects and architects in Beijing, China.

Reprinted with permission from *Topos 51*, July 2005: "Prospective Landscapes", 66–75

58

63

The Art of Survival

Recovering Landscape Architecture

2.1 The Growth Pattern of Taizhou City Based on Ecological Infrastructure

The ASLA Honor Award, Planning and Analysis, 2005

KongjianYu and Dihua Li

The Graduate School of Landscape Architecture, Peking University and Turenscape, Beijing, China

1 Background and Main Issue

The urbanization in China increases about 1 percent annually. Less than 40 percent of the country's 1.3 billion people currently live in urban areas. This number will increase in the next 15 to 20 years to more than 70 percent as cities sprawl at an unprecedented speed. This project is located in the east coast area where the cities grow much faster. In this process, land is overtaken for infrastructure construction and urban development. As a result, the wetlands and terrestrial water systems have been destroyed and polluted. Native habitats and biodiversity are disappearing. The hazards of flooding, drought, and diseases are increasing. At the same time the cultural identity of the landscape is being lost.

Traditionally, greenbelts were planned to stop urban sprawl; but in practice they only are realized on paper. The failure of greenbelt concepts was caused by artificial and arbitrary planning. Serious consideration affecting urban development has been overlooked. New and effective tools have to be developed to address critical issues of sustainable development.

Taizhou is located on the southeast coast of China, with a total area of 9411 square kilometers, and a population of 5.5 million. Only 700,000 people now live in the urban area, and the urban population will increase to 900,000 in 2010, to 1.3 million in 2020, and to 1.5 million in 2030. Though quite rural and agricultural, it is now one of the fastest growing areas in China. This is due to the booming small private industries. With the influence of the monsoon climate and its proximity to the east coast, flooding has been a major hazard. As an adaptation to the stormwater and flood problems, the landscape has been shaped into a unique form featured with a network of water courses that integrate natural water systems, wetlands and artificial ditches. Cultural heritage elements such as bridges, dikes, dams, and vernacular landscapes were also considered in the planning process. This area has long been famous for rice, fisheries and citrus plantations. It is also critical to keep in mind that arable and developable flat area is very limited here.

This water network landscape that has been effective in safeguarding the agricultural processes in the past 1000 years is now facing the challenge of being destroyed by rapid urbanization that began in the early 1990s. The wetlands have been filled. River courses have been straightened and channeled. Unprotected cultural heritage sites have been destroyed, and visual and recreational experiences have been neglected. In addressing ths situation, a project was proposed that established guidelines for controlling urban sprawl and advocating responsible sustainable development that recognizes the limits of our land resources.

2 The Project's Goals and Objectives

The planner's strategic approach takes land as a dynamic living system. The objectives are to create a system that guides urban sprawl. This system is called an ecological infrastructure (EI) that guides urban sprawl. The EI is defined as the structural landscape network that is composed of critical landscape elements and spatial patterns that safeguard the integrity and identity of the natural and cultural landscapes. Sustaining the ecosystem, protecting cultural heritage sites and creating recreational opportunities are also considered in this process.

Comparable to urban infrastructure that provides social and economic services (such as transportation, gas, sewage, etc.) and support urban growth, the EI safeguards ecological services, protects cultural heritage sites, and provides visual and recreational experiences.

3 Targeted Processes Need to be Safeguarded before Urban Growth

Three categories of processes are targeted by the proposed ecological infrastructure:

1 The *abiotic* processes: the main focus is flood control and storm water management.

2 Biotic processes: native species and biodiversity conservation.

3 Cultural processes: including heritage protection and recreational need.

A geographical information system (GIS) was established to store, overlay, and analyze layers of natural, cultural, and social economic data.

4 Defining an Ecological Infrastructure at a Large Scale

The EI is used at the regional scale and examines critical landscape patterns (security patterns) of the targeted processes. The security patterns are composed of elements and spatial positions that are strategically important in safeguarding the different processes of the landscape. Models including suitability analysis, minimum cost distance and surface models were used in the identification of security patterns for the individual processes.

Three security levels—low, medium and high— are used to define the quality of the security patterns in safeguarding each of the targeted processes.

Using an overlaying technique to integrate the security patterns for individual processes, alternatives of regional ecological infrastructure are developed at various quality levels: high, medium and low.

5 Scenarios of Urban Growth Pattern Based on the Regional Ecological Infrastructure

Using the three EI alternatives as a structural framework, scenarios of regional urban growth patterns were simulated using GIS: the adjusted sprawl scenario, the aggregated scenario, and the scattered scenario.

Comparative impact evaluations were made for these scenarios by a planning committee. This committee was composed of decision makers from the city, nation-wide planning experts, Taizhou City government officials from various departments (agriculture, water management, forestry, industry, tourism, finance, transportation, public affairs, security, culture education, tax), village representatives, real estate developers, and investors.

After a long period, the committee selected one of the three urban pattern scenarios. As we expected, the aggregated scenario, which is based on the medium quality EI, was considered the more balanced and less difficult to realize.

6 Pursuing the Legislation Procedure to Protect the EI

Green lines were drawn to define and safeguard the EI protection. These basic green lines are now being presented to the people's congress of Taizhou City for legislation procedure. After being passed by congress, this legislation will become the first of its kind in China that protects the regional ecological infrastructure.

7 Defining Ecological Infrastructure at the Medium Scale

These were based on the aggregated scenario and the green lines of the regional EI. Overall design and management guidelines were developed for the medium quality EI. The green corridors will function as critical EI elements in water management and biodiversity conservation, heritage protection, and recreation. During this process of making the design guidelines, the local community was involved and provided input.

8 New Models of Urban Land Development: Testing Ecological Infrastructure on the Small Scale

A demonstration of the EI occurred at a selected 10-square-kilometer site. Alternative urban development models were designed to test the EI's potential as an urban form. The model utilizes ecosystem services that are safeguarded by the EI and delivered into the urban fabric that minimizes urban sprawl.

These new urban land development models were presented to the developers and investors, and city decision makers. These schemes show how the regional and large scaled EI can be realized at the local scale. The intention was to demonstrate that alternative development approaches are available to maximize the land potential in an ecological and culturally sensitive way.

Project Location: Taizhou City, Zhejiang Province, China

Size: 1356 square kilometers

Owner/Client: The Government of Taizhou City

Design Firm: The Graduate School of Landscape Architecture, Peking University and Turenscape, Beijing, China

Project Directors: Kongjian Yu, Li Dihua

Design Team: Han Xili, Liu Hailong, Li Wei, Zhang Lei, Huang Gang, Chen Jing, Wu Zhiheng, Rainer Schmidt, Antje Stokman

01 The city of Taizhou

urban sprawl indiscriminately
takes over and destroys the
integrity and identity of
the landscape

N

10000   **0**   **10000 Meters**

The simulation of urban sprawl of Taizhou city
based on economic and development oriented model

population (millions)

90		200	
130		250	
150		300	
180		400	

Plate 01 The issue: The urban sprawl of Taizhou city.

02 Objectives and methodology

An ecological infrastructure (EI) is designed to safeguard the natural and cultural processes which are critical to secure the integrity and identity of the landscape, and provide sustainable ecosystem services to the residents.
The EI is constructed, and its ecological services are delivered at three scales: large, medium and small.

Large scale

The regional EI was planned, through the identification of critical landscape patterns (security patterns) for the following processes:
(1) Abiotic processes: flood control and storm water management.
(2) Biotic processes: biodiversity conservation;
(3) Cultural processes: cultural heritage protection and recreation. Alternatives of EI are developed at various security levels: high, medium and low. They are used as structural framework in guiding and framing urban development patterns.

N

| | | 10000 | 0 | 10000 | Meters | | |

population (millions)	
90	200
130	250
150	300

Medium scale

Guidelines were developed for green corridors that function as critical EI elements in water management and biodiversity conservation, recreation, heritage protection and recreation.

Small scale

AT a selected site, alternative urban development models are designed to test the possibility of building an EI based city, in which ecosystem services safeguarded by EI are delivered into the urban fabric.

large scale

Goals and Objectives: Propose an ecological infrastructure to safeguard the integrity and identity of the landscape; and use the EI to guide and frame the urban growth so that the normal unhealthy urban sprawl can be avoided

Targeted processes across the landscape that need to be safeguarded before urban growth

| water process (flood control) | Habitats (biodiversity) | cultural heritage | recreation |

Critical landscape security patterns that can safeguard the above processes

| security patterns for flood control | security patterns for habitats | security patterns for heritage | security patterns for recreation |

To integrate landscape security patterns using overlapping technique to create the overall regional ecological infrastructure (EI) at three security levels

| EI at a lower security level | EI at a medium security level | EI at a higher security |

To develop urban growth scenarios based on the regional EI as proposed above, and carry out a comparative impact analysis for the three urban growth scenarios, and select the more feasible scenarios through a brainstorm among decision makers and experts

| urban growth scenario-1 based on low quality EI | urban growth scenario-2 based on medium quality | urban growth scenario-3 based on high quality EI |

medium scale

To make design guidelines for individual components and especially corridors that make up the selected EI.
The guidelines are made for the functions of flood control and water management, biodiversity protection, cultural heritage protection and recreation needs

small scale

To propose urban land development alternatives following the EI design guidelines to test the possibilities of developing new urban forms based on the EI and avoid the normal urban sprawl pattern, the results are presented to developers and decision makers

| the grid alternative | the slice alternative | the water town alternative |

Plate 02 The objectives and methodology: build an ecological infrastructure (EI) to safeguard the natural, biological and cultural processes and secure the integrity and identity of the landscape, and provide sustaining ecosystem services to the city.

03 Large scale:
flood security patterns

Landscape security patterns are identified using simulating techniques and are planned to retain storm water and avoid flood disaster.
The security patterns are composed of critical lower land, wet land, stream network and lakes. It is assumed that if the flood security patterns are reserved, the concrete dams and banks can be avoided.

flood is a frequent
hazard in Taizhou

high rised bank was usually
built to keep off flood

use of wet land, lower land
and stream network to construct
flood security patterns

existing water system

+

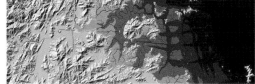

surface flow and risk of tides

+

potential wet land where
surface flow retain

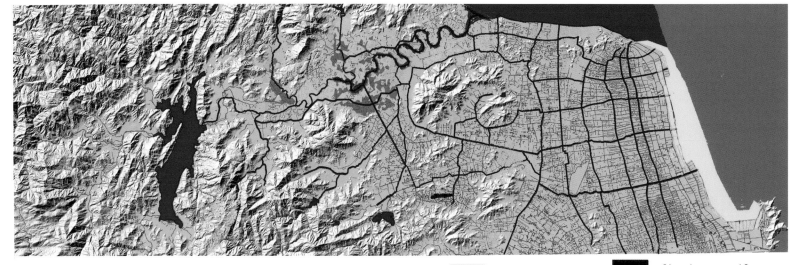

N

10000   0   10000 **Meters**

The potential of flood hazard

built area

∿ 1st grade stream

∿ 2nd grade stream

⋀ 3rd grade stream

flood every 10 years

flood every 20 years

flood every 50 years

beach wetland

Plate 03 Large scale: security patterns of flood control.

04 Large scale:
security pattens for biodiversity

Using index species and based on land cover maps and terrain, existing and potential habitats are identified. In addition, spatial relationships between habitats are also simulated using GIS model, and landscape ecological principles.

Platalea minor   Larus saundersi   Syrmaticus elliot   Neofeis nebulosa

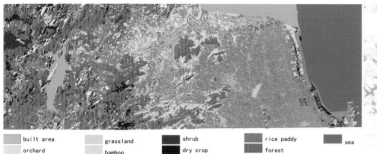 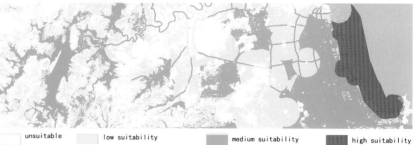

built area	unsuitable
orchard	low suitability
grassland	medium suitability
bamboo	high suitability
shrub	
dry crop	
rice paddy	
forest	
sea	

land cover

habitat suitability analysis

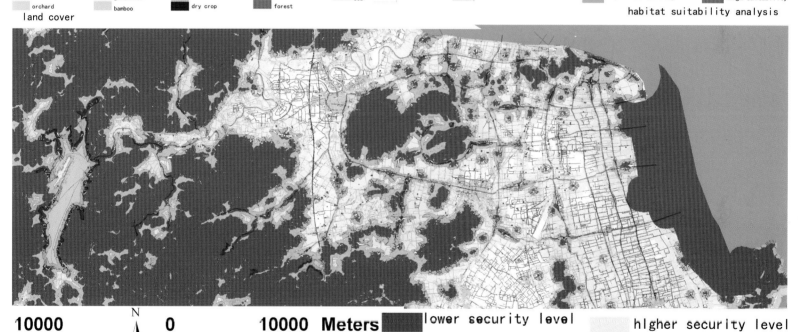

10000   N   0   10000 **Meters**

lower security level
medium security level
higher security level
built area

The security pattern for biodiversity conservation

Plate 04 Large scale: security patterns for biodiversity conservation.

69

05 Large scale:
Planned ecological network
for biodiversity

Using landscape ecological principles, an ecological
network was designed In this map, strategic points
and critical areas were also identified for
special management attention and design specifications

under pass for species and flows

ecological bridge for animals

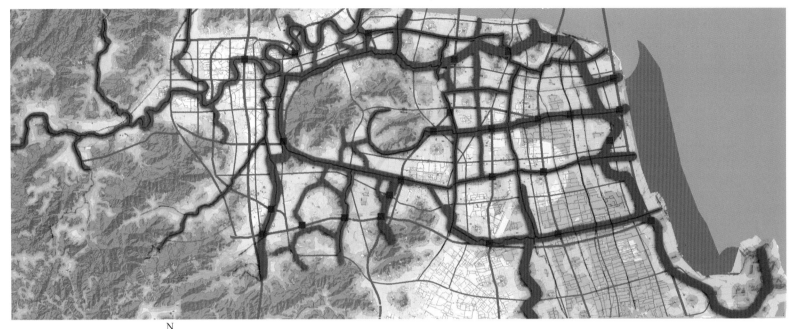

10000 Meters   N   0

The ecological network
indicating critical sections
and points that need special
attention

built area	
potential corridors	
corridors need to be built	
planned road	
strategic points	

source(core habitats)

areas at lower security

areas at medium security

area at higher security

Plate 05 Large scale: Planned landscape security pattern for biodiversity conservation.

75-06 Large scale:
Security pattern for cultural heritage

Both inscribed historical sites and vernacular cultural heritages are identified as the sources for protection. Based on distance and landscape resistance (associated with terrain and land cover), linkages among heritage sites were built. A heritage network was built for education and recreation purposes.

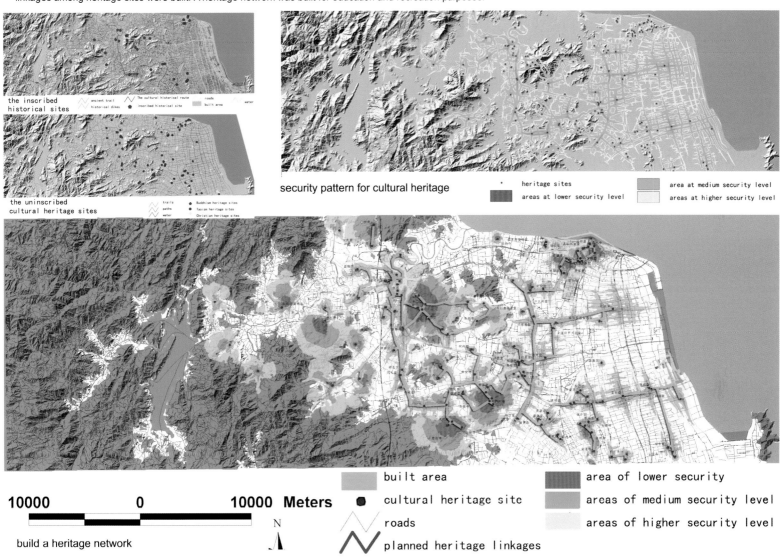

the inscribed historical sites

the uninscribed cultural heritage sites

security pattern for cultural heritage

10000   0   10000 **Meters**

N

build a heritage network

built area
cultural heritage site
roads
planned heritage linkages

area of lower security
areas of medium security level
areas of higher security level

Plate 06 Large scale: security pattern for cultural heritage protection.

07 Large scale: security pattern for recreation

Landscape elements including wetland, forests, water features, and cultural heritage sites were identified as sources for recreation. The security pattern for recreation landscape was identified according to the recreational values of theses resources and their accessibility. Based on their spatial relationships, a recreational landscape network was designed.

security pattern
for recreation

• heritage site

recreational landscape elements
(hill, forest, water, wet land)

■ area at lower security level
■ area at medium security level
□ area at higher security level

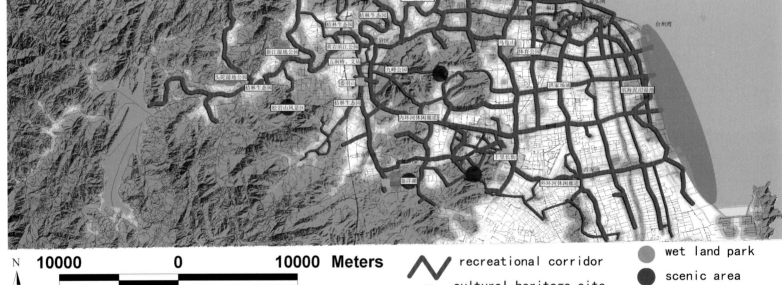

N
10000   0   10000 Meters
Λ

buid a network for landscape recreation

∿ recreational corridor

▫ cultural heritage site

● wet land park
● scenic area
● citrus orchard

Plate 07 Large scale: security pattern for recreation.

08 Large scale:
Regional ecological infrastructure

The regional ecological infrastructure (EI) was an integration of security patterns and plans for flood control, biodiversity conservation, cultural heritage protection and recreation. Three alternatives of EI were developed corresponding to high, medium and low security levels. They will be used to guide and frame regional urban development pattern.

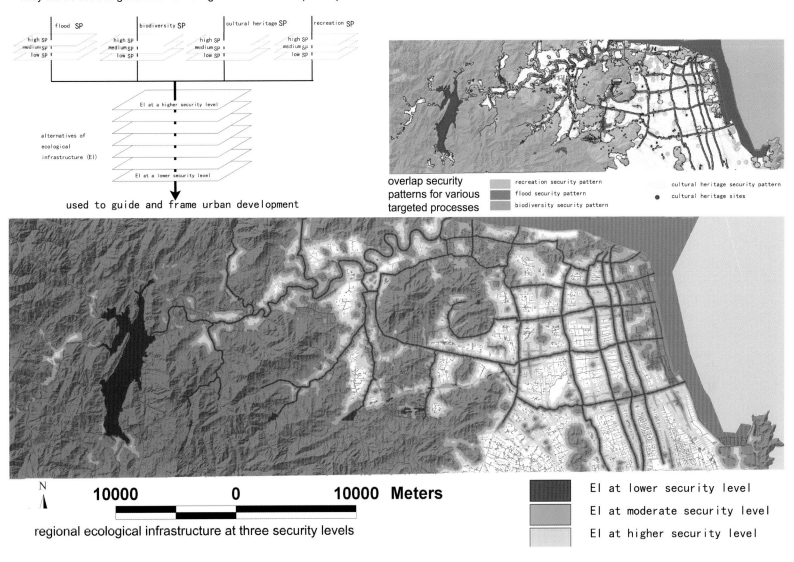

used to guide and frame urban development

overlap security patterns for various targeted processes

recreation security pattern
flood security pattern
biodiversity security pattern

cultural heritage security pattern
cultural heritage sites

N

10000   0   10000 Meters

regional ecological infrastructure at three security levels

EI at lower security level
EI at moderate security level
EI at higher security level

Plate 08 Large scale: overall regional ecological infrastructure.

09 Urban growth scenario: the adjusted sprawl
the urban pattern based on the EI at a lower security level

At a lower security level, the ecological infrastructure (EI) will allow the city to accommodate a maximum population of 5 millions, and yet still keep a minimum critical landscape structure to safeguard the natural and cultural processes that are strategically important for the integrity and identity of the landscape, and provide minimum ecosystem services.

According to an independent projection, the city will have a population of 1.30million in 2020,and 1.5 in 2030, which are much lower than the city will be able to accommodate if it is wisely arranged. Our analysis therefore suggested to the decision makers that: a sustainable development can be achieved by wisely arranged urban development and land use pattern. The protection and natural processes, biodiversity, the protection of cultural heritage and recreational resources does not mean the sacrifice of urban development. Here, ecological infrastructure is the key.

The advantages of the adjusted sprawl scenario lies in its efficiency in urban development. The EI plays a connecting element for cycling and pedestrian, as well as provide recreation and other ecosystem services.

	environmental	cultural and social	economical
impact analysis (in brief)	fair, better than usual sprawl urban form	good, cultural heritages are well protected, good accessibility to recreational resources, good sense of urban community	most efficient, urban land and infrastructure is most economically used.

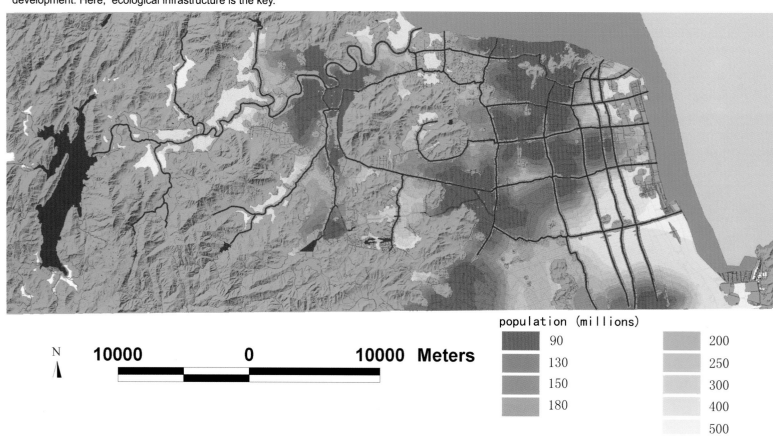

population (millions)

90	200
130	250
150	300
180	400
	500

N

10000   0   10000 Meters

Plate 09 Urban growth scenario: the adjusted sprawl. At a lower security level, the EI will allow the city to accommodate a maximum population of 5 million, and yet still keep a minimum critical landscape structure in safeguarding the integrity and identity of the landscape, and provide minimum ecosystem services.

10 Urban growth scenario: the aggregated the urban pattern based on the EI at a medium security level

At a medium security level, the ecological infrastructure (EI) will allow the city to accommodate a maximum population of 3 millions (still can accommodate even the highest population projection in the next century), and keep a good landscape structure to safeguard the natural and cultural processes that are strategically important for the integrity and identity of the landscape, and provide sufficient ecosystem services.

The advantages for this scenario lies in its harmonious state integrating natural systems protection, cultural and social benefits and economic efficiency.

	environmental	cultural and social	economical
impact analysis (brief)	good, better than both usual sprawl urban form and the adjusted sprawl urban form	very well protected cultural heritages, good accessibility to recreational resources, good sense of urban community	highly efficient, urban land and infrastructure is most economically used.

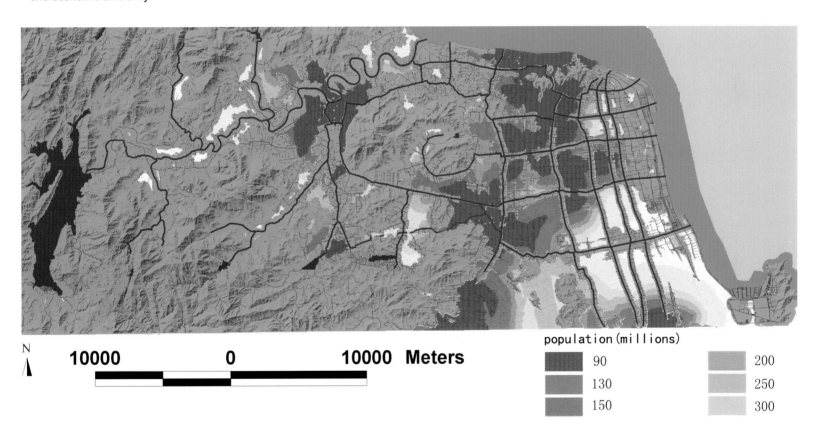

N

10000   **0**   **10000 Meters**

population(millions)

90		200	
130		250	
150		300	

Plate 10 Urban growth scenario: the aggregated urban pattern based on the EI at a medium security level.

11 Urban growth scenario: the scattered the urban pattern based on the EI at a higher security level

At a higher security level, the ecological infrastructure (EI) will allow the city to accommodate a maximum population of 1.5 millions (still can accommodate the highest population projection in the 2030), and keep a possible the best landscape structure to safeguard the natural and cultural processes that are strategically important for the integrity and identity of the landscape, and provide the most possible ecosystem services.

The main disadvantage of the scattered pattern lies in its potential inefficient urban land use and uneconomic infrastructures development.

	environmental	cultural and social	economical
impact analysis (brief)	Best in the protection of natural processes, provide best ecosystem services	well protected cultural heritages and mostly accessible to recreational resources, but less sense of urban community	less efficient, urban land and infrastructure use due to the further apart development pattern.

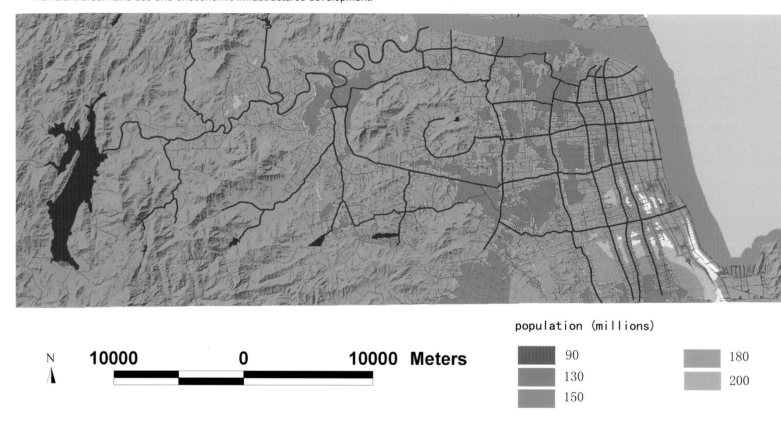

population (millions)

N

10000   0   10000 Meters

90	180
130	200
150	

Plate 11 Urban growth scenario: the scattered urban pattern based on the EI at a higher security level.

12 Medium scale: EI corridor design

Design guidelines are made for individual corridors and areas that compose regional EI. Among the three scenarios of EI, the EI at the medium security level was selected, only one of the corridor is shown on this board, which has multiple functions for water management and flood control, biodiversity conservation, cultural heritage protection and recreation.

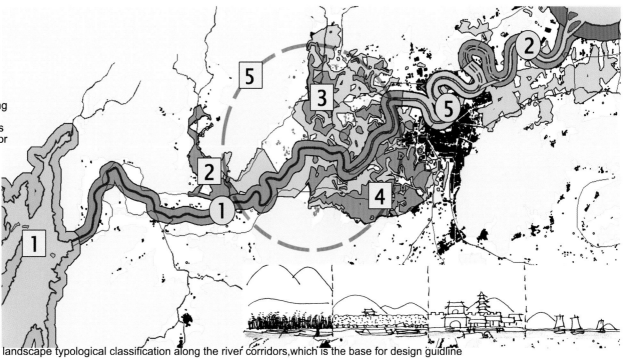

flood security patters at three levels

vegetation along the river corridor

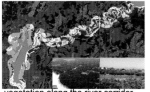

productive agricultural land

vernacular landscape types

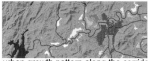

urban growth pattern along the corridor

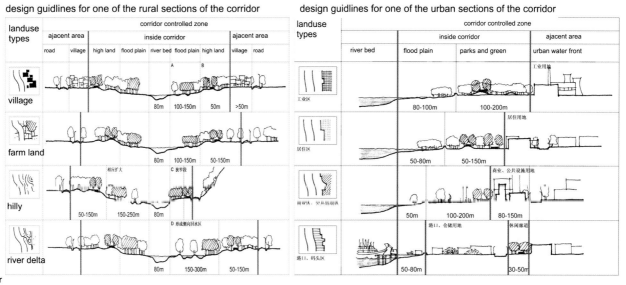

landscape typological classification along the river corridors, which is the base for design guidline

design guidlines for one of the rural sections of the corridor

landuse types	corridor controlled zone							
	ajacent area		inside corridor					ajacent area
	road	village	high land	flood plain	river bed	flood plain	high land	village	road
village					80m	100-150m	50m	>50m	
farm land					80m	100-150m	50-150m		
hilly				50-150m	150-250m	80m			
river delta					80m	150-300m	50-150m		

design guidlines for one of the urban sections of the corridor

landuse types	corridor controlled zone			
		inside corridor		ajacent area
	river bed	flood plain	parks and green	urban water front
工业区		80-100m	100-200m	工业用地
居住区		50-80m	50-150m	居住用地
商业状、灵共结合区		50m	100-200m	80-150m	商业、公共设施用地
港口、码头区		50-80m		30-50m	港口、仓储用地 休闲应道

Plate 12 Medium scale: EI corridor design guidelines.

77

13 Small scale:
the slice alternative

A site of ten square kilometers was selected to test the
possibilities of new urban development patterns based on
EI. Three alternatives are proposed: the SLICE, GRID and
WATER TOWN.

The slice alternative let the ecological services from the
regional EI delivered through corridors and penetrate
into the urban fabric just like vegetable layers in a sandwich.

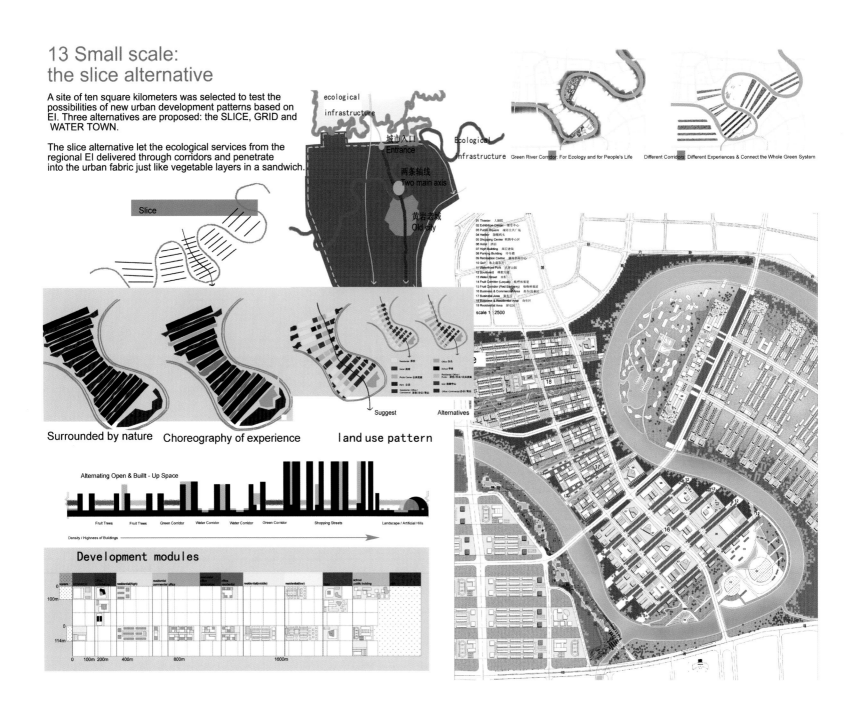

Surrounded by nature   Choreography of experience   land use pattern

Plate 13 Small scale: the slice alternative. A site of ten square kilometers was selected to test the possibilities of new urban development patterns based on EI. Three alternatives are proposed: the SLICE, GRID and WATER TOWN. The slice alternative allowed the ecological services from the regional EI to be delivered through corridors and penetrate into the urban fabric just like vegetable layers in a sandwich.

14 Small scale:
The grid alternative

Use a grid system of green in steady of roads to deliver the ecological services into the urban fabric

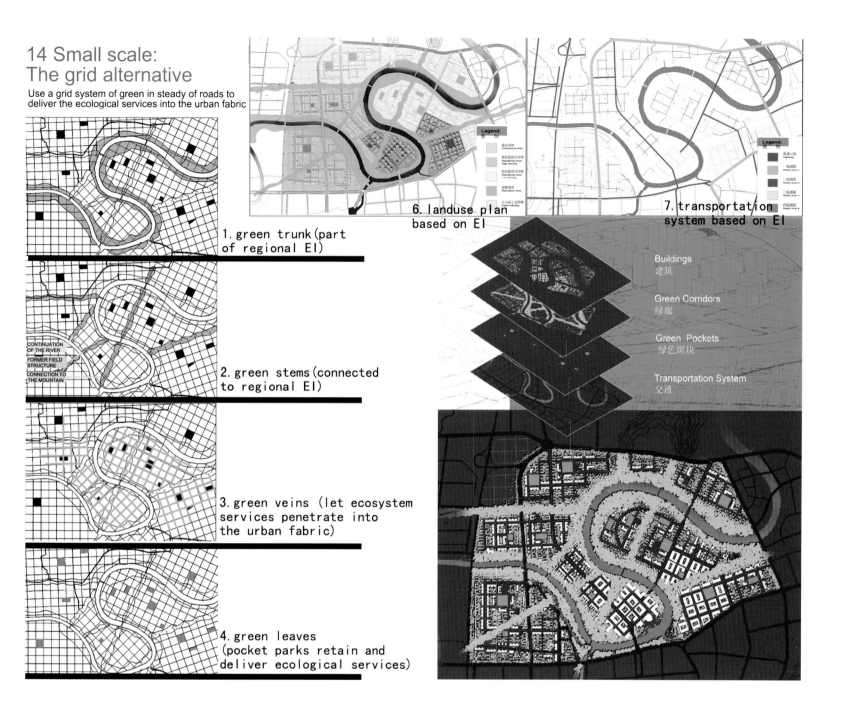

1. green trunk (part of regional El)

2. green stems (connected to regional El)

CONTINUATION OF THE RIVER
FORMER FIELD STRUCTURE
CONNECTION TO THE MOUNTAIN

3. green veins (let ecosystem services penetrate into the urban fabric)

4. green leaves (pocket parks retain and deliver ecological services)

6. landuse plan based on El

7. transportation system based on El

Buildings
建筑

Green Corridors
绿廊

Green Pockets
绿色斑块

Transportation System
交通

Plate 14 Small scale: The grid alternative. A grid system of green instead of roads to deliver the ecological services into the urban fabric.

flood is to be avoided through retaining and diverging water, but not by channelizing and daming. Let one river become ten streams and let the ecological services from the EI penetrate into the urban fabric and individual households.

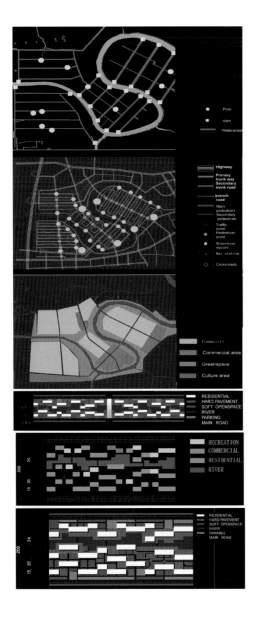

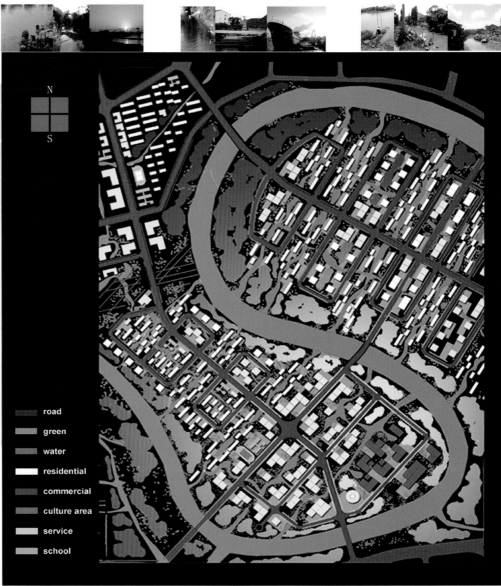

Plate 15 Small scale: The water town alternative. Flood hazard is to be avoided through retaining and diverging water, but not by channelizing and damming. Allow one river to become ten streams and let the ecological services from the EI penetrate into the urban fabric and individual households.

2.2 Rescuing a Village: Magang Landscape Planning

Kongjian Yu, Dihua Li, Xili Han

The Graduate School of Landscape Architecture, Peking University and Turenscape, Beijing, China

1 Background and Key Issues: Villages in Danger

The process of urban sprawl in China has overtaken hundreds of thousands of native rural habitats. This pattern of urbanization that pushes the boundary of the city fringe has caused the destruction of the cultural heritage of local vernacular landscapes and villages that have developed over several millennia at the fringe of urban spaces, destroying hundreds and thousands of years of history.

Only a limited number of nationally designated historical townships and villages have survived this overwhelming process of urbanization. Most villages and cultural landscapes have been bulldozed in a short period of time, only to be replaced with new urban communities.

Further, this process causes existing communities to be relocated to new residential developments. The lack of cultural sensitivity and value systems toward preservation and conservation causes serious ecological, cultural, and social impacts including:

1 Destruction of the physical landscape

2 Destruction of local heritage and resulting loss of the cultural identity of both the local and regional landscape

3 Destruction of the sense of place

4 Destruction of social structure and community fabric.

Magang is a village of more than 7000 residents, located on an island at the fringe of Shunde, one of the fastest developing cities in southern China's Guangdong Province. The village occupies a total area of 12 square kilometers, and has existed for more than 400 years. The area's regional landscape was historically known for its combination of banana plantations and fishponds, an endangered cultural landscape that is rapidly disappearing. The former masterplan for this area suggested the destruction of Magang village in favor of new urban development. The landscape architect was invited to give a second opinion, and formulated a modified masterplan that was preservation-oriented and integrated the Magang cultural landscape.

Magang is a typical example of China's endangered villages. This submission suggests an alternative approach to urbanization that affects villages at the fringe of major cities.

2 Objectives and Methodology

As a guiding planning principle for the project, the consultant team established the village as a living organism. The main strategy is preservation-oriented. At the same time, the cultural heritage of the village should not be perceived to be a burden on Magang's urbanization. Rather, preservation of this heritage should be considered a positive agent for urbanization by increasing the sense of cultural and social identity and providing recreational and cultural tourism opportunities. The intention is to provide a grassroots system of social and spiritual networking in the proposed urbanized community.

We recommend these objectives be achieved by the following steps:

1 Inventory. Represent and identify the critical landscape elements and structure, noting the strategically important ecological, historical, cultural, spiritual and social processes.

2 Analyze, evaluate and develop design guidelines that are sensitive to cultural heritage and the existing landscape elements and structure

3 Networking and patchworking. Integrate strategic landscape patterns into a network of both daily experience and tourism. This network should be flexible to allow for change.

3 Analysis: Critical Processes and Landscape Patterns for Magang

Five landscape patterns and associated processes are critical to maintaining Magang's historic integrity:

1 Terrain and water and their ecological and cultural meanings: the significant relationship between *feng shui*, terrain, and water had originally played an important role in the setting and design of Magang. These features must be maintained in the new design. The evaluation of the terrain and water for planning purposes is based on the following criteria:

• Ecological values (including biodiversity and regenerative capability)

• Cultural values (*feng shui* meanings, traditional belief systems, organic agriculture)

• Environmental values (such as water quality)

Based on a sifting process, we developed an integrated map of Magang's most valued terrain and water. The protection of the village's macro landscape setting is critical to maintaining a sense of place and giving Magang its identity, as well as to protecting a healthy environment and ecology.

2 Open space system and cultural social processes: villagers from Magang and its vicinity gather year round for various activities. Thousands of people visit Magang to celebrate all kinds of festivals such dragon dancing, Buddha's birthday, Chinese lunar new year, and moon festivals. Every day, chance encounters and social gatherings, such as group television viewing or sipping morning tea together, occur in public spaces. These activities are lively aspects of the village, and are set in certain open spaces that are scattered throughout the village. It is critical that these spaces be preserved in Magang's new plan.

Three levels of open spaces are categorized in Magang: the village level, the extended family level, and neighborhood level. These different levels of open spaces exist in combination with ancestral temples, Buddhist temples, shrines to various spirits, sacred trees, ponds, wells, as well as sports and recreational facilities.

The evaluation of these public spaces has been based on the following criteria:

• Accessibility

• Influential sphere

• Physical quality

• Importance of activities

• Tree quality

Based on a sifting process, we developed an integrated map of Magang's most valued public spaces. The protection and improvement of this open space system are critical to maintaining Magang's many cultural and social activities.

3 Religious buildings and spiritual activities: the social structure of Magang is based on the patriarchal clan system and family lineage. There are four dormant families, namely the Feng, Li, She, and Luo families. Each of these families has ancestral temples that are the spiritual centers of the village and the core of Magang's social chain. In addition, Buddhism, Taoism, Confucianism, as well as local religious beliefs, all coexist. Each has separate or combined temples and shrines.

These religious sites are always associated with some *feng shui* landscape elements such a hills, water, and trees. They are usually at the center of various formal and informal gatherings in Magang's social spaces.

The evaluation of these religious buildings has been based on the following criteria:

• The historical value of the buildings

• The religious sphere of the temples and shrines

Based on a sifting process, we developed an integrated map of Magang's most and highly valued religious buildings. Protection and improvement of these religious buildings is important in establishing a moral and harmonious society at the grass roots level.

4 Street networks and connectivity: families and individuals are closely connected in Magang through a network of pedestrian streets and lanes. This street network also renders cultural and religious places easily accessible to villagers. The most heavily trafficked streets must be kept safe and highly accessible to the community. This will remain important even after the village is integrated into the new urban fabric.

This network is now facing development challenges. Wide roads are already planned or are under construction, while the pedestrian streets are also facing the pressure to be widened, which can only be accomplished by taking down the old and historic buildings. Thus, Magang's connected street network is being disrupted by increased traffic and road construction.

The evaluation of the street network has been based on the following criteria:

• Connection to the natural landscape settings of Magang

• Connection to highly valued open spaces and religious buildings

• Visual quality

Based on a sifting process, the integrated map indicates the most valued and highly valued streets. The protection and improvement of this street network is important to keeping Magang alive.

5 Residence and individual buildings and cultural identity: the Magang village is a patchwork of individual buildings of different ages, forms, locations, and meanings. Some are critical to safeguarding the cultural and visual identity and integrity of the village. The identification and careful preservation of these critical buildings is therefore important. The traditional buildings are usually in a courtyard form and one to two storys tall. Newly constructed buildings are normally three to four storys tall and are generally featureless and nondescript.

The evaluation criteria of Magang's residential and individual buildings includes:

• Physical quality and compatibility with vernacular architecture

• Historical and cultural significance

• Physical status (such as construction quality)

Based on a sifting process, the integrated map indicates the most valued and highly valued residencial buildings. The protection and improvement of these residences is important to keeping Magang's visual and cultural integrity and identity.

The integrated strategic landscape pattern is developed by overlapping these five highly valued landscape patterns. This pattern is the basis for Magang's preservation and new development. The most valued areas will not be developed, while moderately valued areas will undergo controlled development. Less valued areas are encouraged for new development.

4 Planning Strategies to Rescue Magang: Networking and Patchworking

In order to keep Magang alive while allowing for new urban development, two strategies will be pursued:

1 Networking: overlaying and integrating the critical landscape patterns, strategically important to safeguarding ecological, cultural, spiritual, and social processes, will protect Magang's cultural landscape. This landscape network is a minimum baseline for the protection of Magang, which not only will maintain the integrity of Magang, but will also act as an experiential route for tourists. It is a tie between history and future, between the old village and the new urban community, between the land and people, and between the native residents and new immigrants. Tourist facilities and environmental interpretive displays can also be allocated along this network.

2 Patchworking: as an alternative to the conventional approach of urban development by the total removal of villages, the patching approach suggests the integration of the existing village landscape with the new development. This interwoven fabric creates social, cultural and spatial diversity that is the single most important factor in bringing vitality to the city.

One section of Magang village, where indiscriminate development has just begun, is taken as a model for a more detailed design of patching.

5 A New Urban Community with an Aged Grassroot System

This proposed alternative planning approach of networking and patching may bring vitality to the new city and future development of the site. This approach allows protection and integration of the existing social, cultural, and spiritual systems, while also creating an urbanized community of ecological integrity, historical continuity, cultural identity, and social harmony.

Project Location: Shunde, Guangdong Province, China

Size: 8.3 square kilometers

Owner/Client: The Government of Shunde City

Design Firm: The Graduate School of Landscape Architecture, Peking University and Turenscape, Beijing, China

Project Director: Kongjian Yu, Li Dihua

Design Team: Han Xili, Ruan Bo, Pei Dan, Deng Xichun, Huang Jianwen, Chen Biyun

01 A DISAPPEARING VILLAGE

1.LOCATION

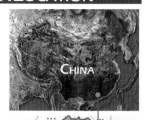

CHINA

GUANGDONG

MAGANG

THE VILLAGE OF MAGANG

2.BACKGROUND

China's overwhelming urban sprawl has wiped out hundreds of thousands of villages at the outskirts of cities. Historical cultural landscapes have been bulldozed overnight and replaced with totally new urban communities. Native inhabitants are often relocated to utterly new residential settlements. This is having serious ecological, cultural and social impacts, including:

(1) Destruction of the ecological land-scape,
(2) Destruction of cultural identity of the local and regional landscape,
(3) Destruction of the sense of place,
(4) Destruction of social structure and community ties

The urbanization process in the Pearl River Delta

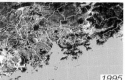

1990

1995

Magang is wiped out in a con-ventional development plan

3.INTRODUCTION OF MAGANG

Magang: is a typically en-dangered village, where:

(1) A meaningful and careful-ly maintained natural setting has become fragmented;
(2) Cultural landscapes of more than 400 years' history will be wiped out;
(3) The open space system and traditional residences that create cultural identity and a sense of place are going to be destroyed;
(4) Numerous ancestral and religious temples that create spiritual integrity and a har-monious society are going to be removed.

Magan is a typical endangered village. This submission suggests an alternative approach to the urbanization of villages at the outskirts of main cities..

Plate 01 The issue and background: urban sprawl in China has been wiping out hundreds of thousands of native villages at the fringe of cities. Magan is one such typical endangered village.

02 OBJECTIVES & METHODOLOGY

1.OBJECTIVES

(1) Take Magang as a living organism with its history and integrity, and integrate it into the new urban organism.

(2)Take Magang as a positive agent for the process of urbanization by increasing cultural and social diversity and identity, providing tourism opportunities, and consolidating grassroots of social and spiritual network in the community.

2.METHODOLOGY

(1) Represent and identify the critical landscape elements and structures necessary to safeguarding the ecological, historical, cultural, spiritual and social systems in Magang strategically important to keeping the village alive.

(2) Evaluate and develop design guidelines for the existing landscape elements and structure, so that they may efficiently safeguard ecological, cultural, spiritual and social systems, while leaving land for new development.

(3) Take the planning strategies of networking and patching: This integrated strategic network must be preserved and/or changed carefully during the process of new development, to be interwoven into the new urban community.

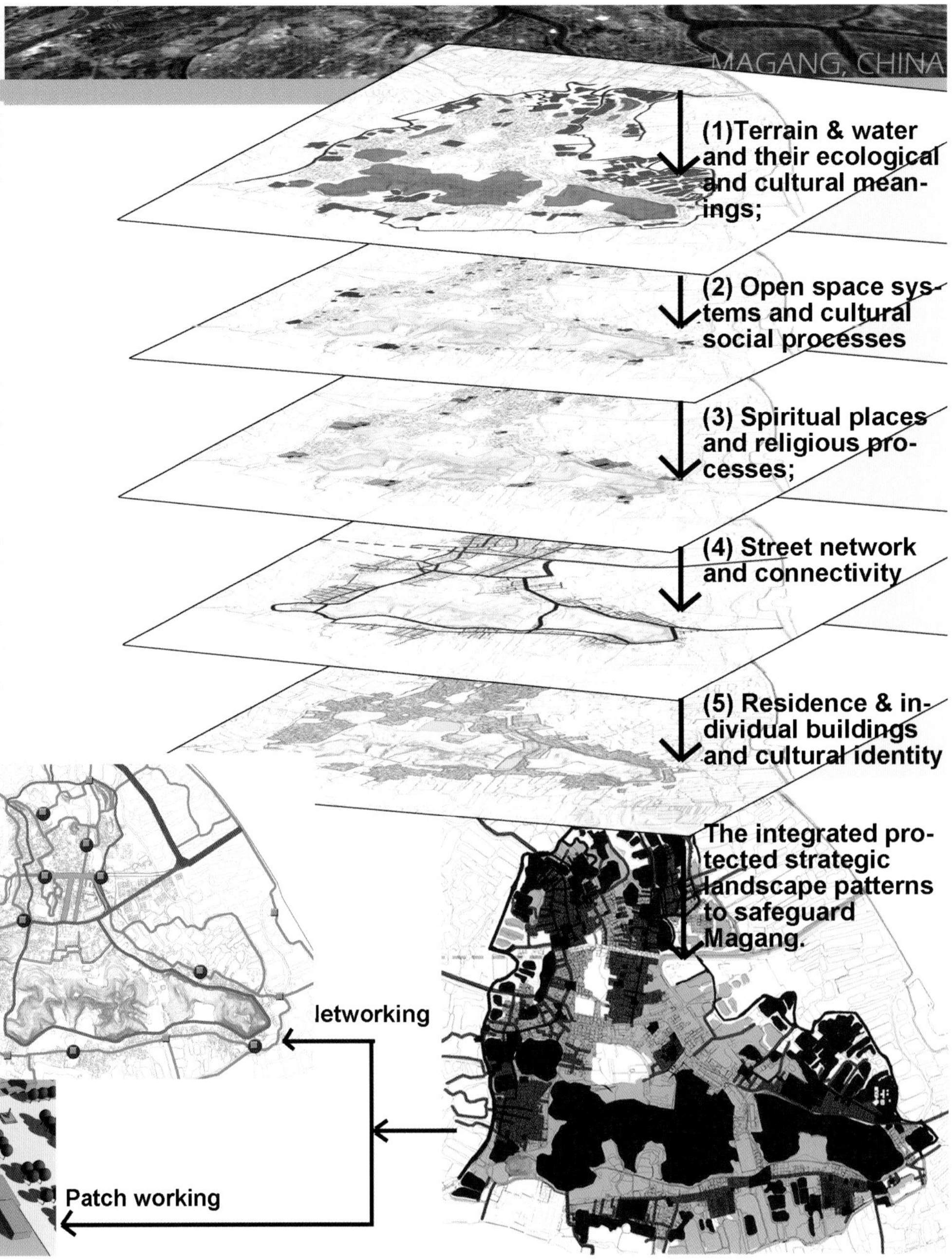

(1)Terrain & water and their ecological and cultural meanings;

(2) Open space systems and cultural social processes

(3) Spiritual places and religious processes;

(4) Street network and connectivity

(5) Residence & individual buildings and cultural identity

The integrated protected strategic landscape patterns to safeguard Magang.

letworking

Patch working

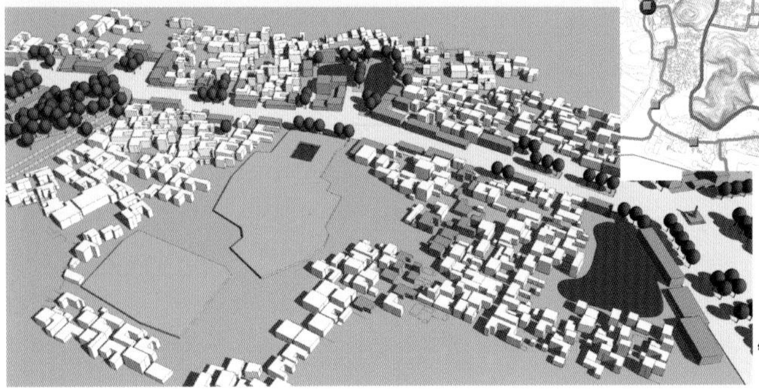

Plate 02 Objectives and methodology: securing strategic cultural landscape patterns and features while allowing maximum landscape change for new development.

03 TERRAIN & WATER

1. REPRESENTATION

■ Terrain and water (as Magang is rich with *feng-shui* meanings and ecological functions);

■ Banana and fish ponds plantations exist only in this region and is a part of the productive agricultural heritage.

■ Water courses system dug to drain the water in the Pearl River Dealt region is a type of ecologically and environmentally significant man-made wetland system.

■ All these critical cultural landscapes are now facing destruction due to the rise in urban development.

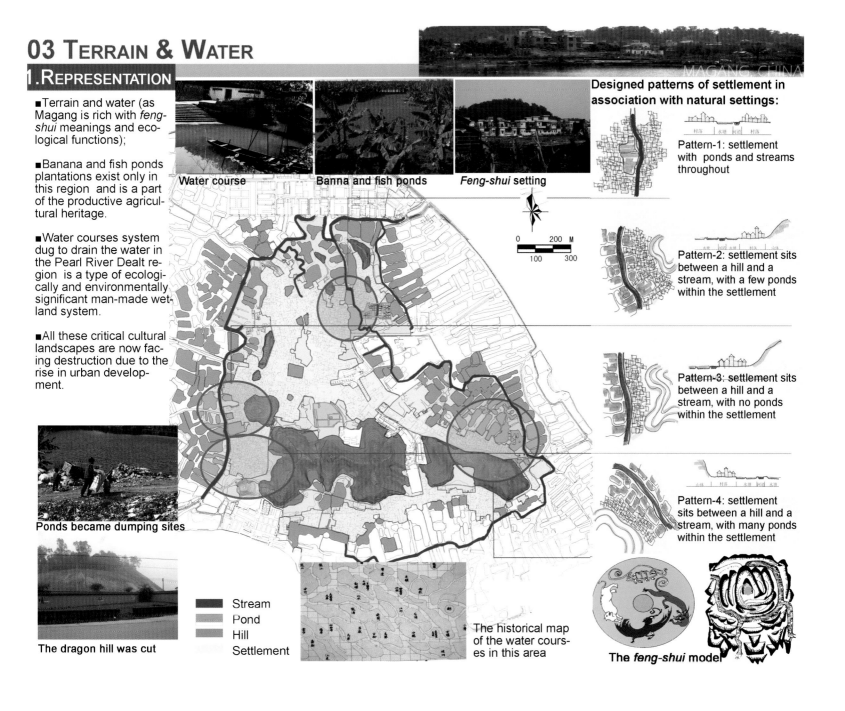

Water course

Banna and fish ponds

Feng-shui setting

Ponds became dumping sites

The dragon hill was cut

Stream
Pond
Hill
Settlement

The historical map of the water courses in this area

Designed patterns of settlement in association with natural settings:

Pattern-1: settlement with ponds and streams throughout

Pattern-2: settlement sits between a hill and a stream, with a few ponds within the settlement

Pattern-3: settlement sits between a hill and a stream, with no ponds within the settlement

Pattern-4: settlement sits between a hill and a stream, with many ponds within the settlement

The *feng-shui* model

0   200 M
100   300

Plate 03 Identification of the strategic pattern of macro-terrain and water settings in relation to village.

04 TERRAIN & WATER

2.EVALUATION

3.DESIGN GUIDELINES

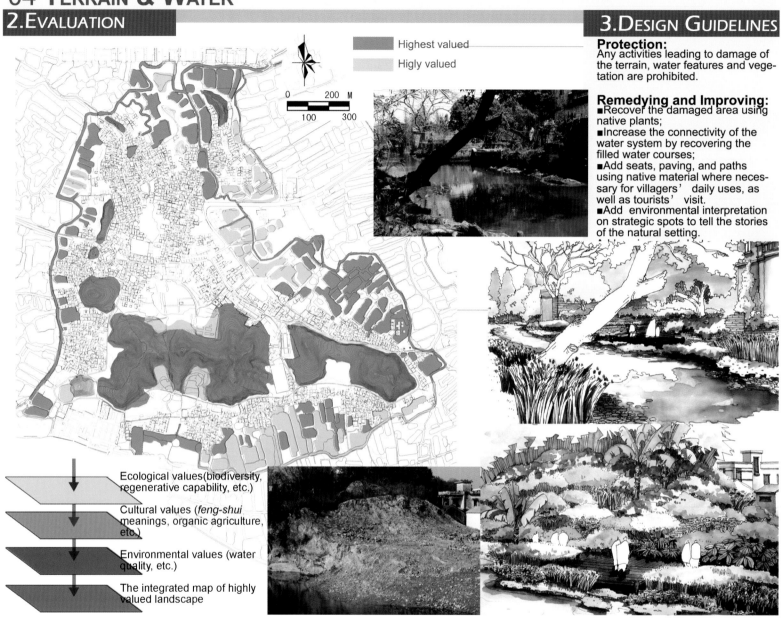

Highest valued

Higly valued

0   200 M
100   300

Ecological values(biodiversity, regenerative capability, etc.)

Cultural values (*feng-shui* meanings, organic agriculture, etc.)

Environmental values (water quality, etc.)

The integrated map of highly valued landscape

Protection:
Any activities leading to damage of the terrain, water features and vegetation are prohibited.

Remedying and Improving:
■Recover the damaged area using native plants;
■Increase the connectivity of the water system by recovering the filled water courses;
■Add seats, paving, and paths using native material where necessary for villagers' daily uses, as well as tourists' visit.
■Add environmental interpretation on strategic spots to tell the stories of the natural setting.

Plate 04 Evaluation and development of design guidelines for the overall terrain and water, to safeguard the ecological security and cultural meaning of the macro-landscape.

05 OPEN SPACE

1. REPRESENTATION

■Villagers from Magang and its vicinity gather year-round for various activities . Thousands of people come Magang to celebrate all kinds of festivals, such as: dragon dancing, the Buddha´s birthday, the Chinese lunar new year as well as daily meetings and gatherings.

■All of these activities are among the most lively part of village life, and are attached to certain public spaces that are scattered all over the village in an hierarchical system.

■Three levels of open spaces are categorized:
 Village level;
 Neighborhood level, and;
 Extended family level.

■Open spaces exist in combination with: ancestral temples, Buddhist temples, shrines of various spirits, sacred trees, pond, wells, as well as sports and recreational facilities.

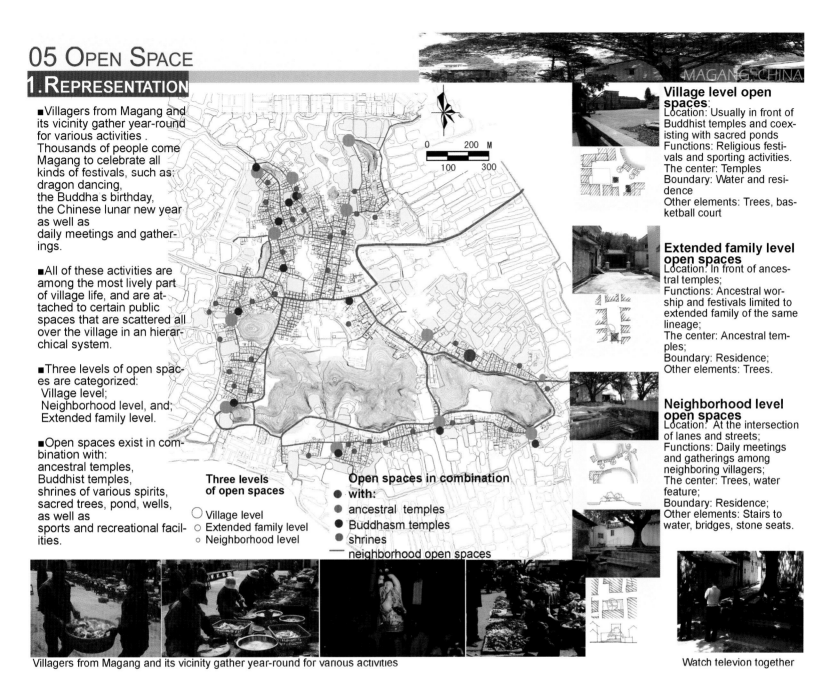

Three levels of open spaces

○ Village level
○ Extended family level
○ Neighborhood level

Open spaces in combination with:
● ancestral temples
● Buddhasm temples
● shrines
— neighborhood open spaces

Village level open spaces:
Location: Usually in front of Buddhist temples and coexisting with sacred ponds
Functions: Religious festivals and sporting activities.
The center: Temples
Boundary: Water and residence
Other elements: Trees, basketball court

Extended family level open spaces
Location: In front of ancestral temples;
Functions: Ancestral worship and festivals limited to extended family of the same lineage;
The center: Ancestral temples;
Boundary: Residence;
Other elements: Trees.

Neighborhood level open spaces
Location: At the intersection of lanes and streets;
Functions: Daily meetings and gatherings among neighboring villagers;
The center: Trees, water feature;
Boundary: Residence;
Other elements: Stairs to water, bridges, stone seats.

Villagers from Magang and its vicinity gather year-round for various activities

Watch televion together

Plate 05 Identification of strategic open space within the village.

2.EVALUATION

3.DESIGN GUIDELINES

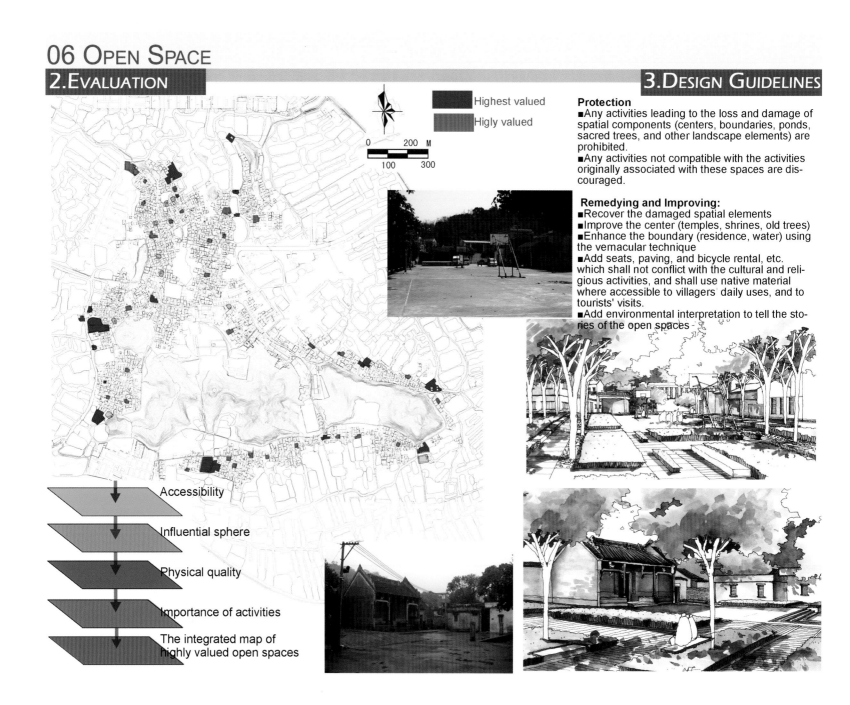

Highest valued

Higly valued

0   200 M

100   300

Accessibility

Influential sphere

Physical quality

Importance of activities

The integrated map of highly valued open spaces

Protection
■Any activities leading to the loss and damage of spatial components (centers, boundaries, ponds, sacred trees, and other landscape elements) are prohibited.
■Any activities not compatible with the activities originally associated with these spaces are discouraged.

Remedying and Improving:
■Recover the damaged spatial elements
■Improve the center (temples, shrines, old trees)
■Enhance the boundary (residence, water) using the vernacular technique
■Add seats, paving, and bicycle rental, etc. which shall not conflict with the cultural and religious activities, and shall use native material where accessible to villagers' daily uses, and to tourists' visits.
■Add environmental interpretation to tell the stories of the open spaces

Plate 06 Evaluatation and development of design guidelines for an open space system within village to safeguard cultural and social meanings.

07 RELIGIOUS BUILDINGS

1. REPRESENTATION

The social structure of Magang is based on the patriarchal clan system and family lineage. There are four dormant families, namely the Feng, Li, She and Luo families. Each of these families has ancestral temples that become the spiritual centers of the village and the core of the social chain.

In addition, Buddhism, Taoism, Confucianism and local religious beliefs all coexist and have their separate or combined temples and shrines. Identification and preservation of these religious buildings are important in creating a moral and harmonious society at the grassroots.

These religious buildings are always associated with key feng-shui landscape elements such a hills, water and trees. They usually become the center of various levels of open spaces.

The various relationships between religious buildings and natural settings (hills and water)

Religious temples
Ancestral temples
Shrines of spirits

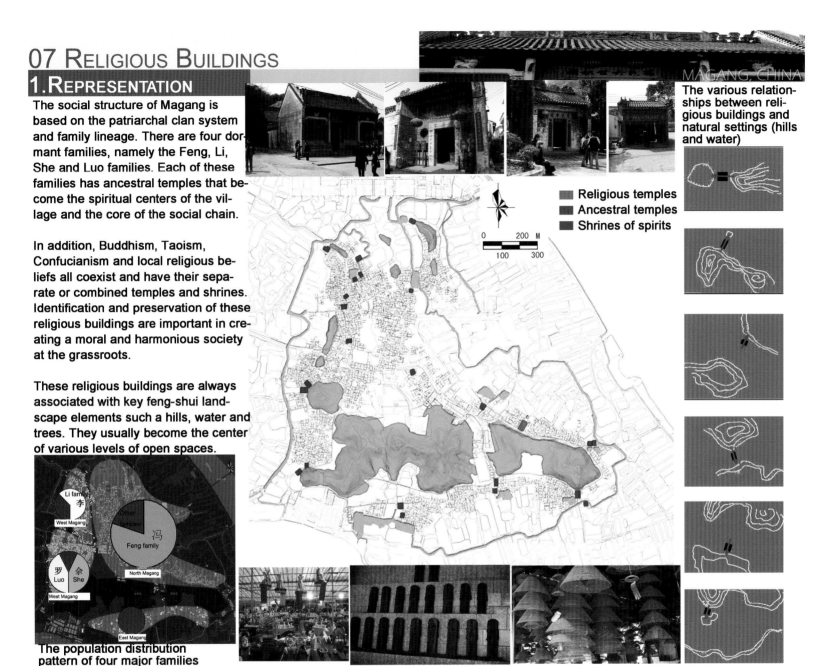

The population distribution pattern of four major families

Plate 07 Identification of strategic religious buildings.

08 RELIGIOUS PLACES

2.EVALUATION

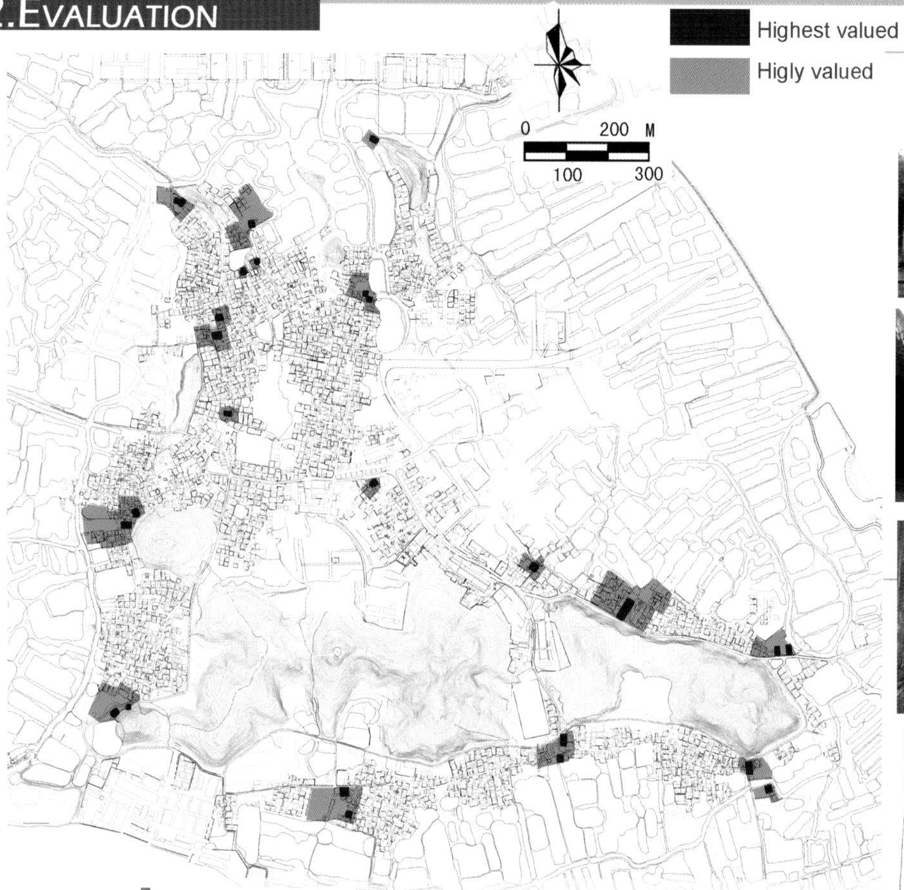

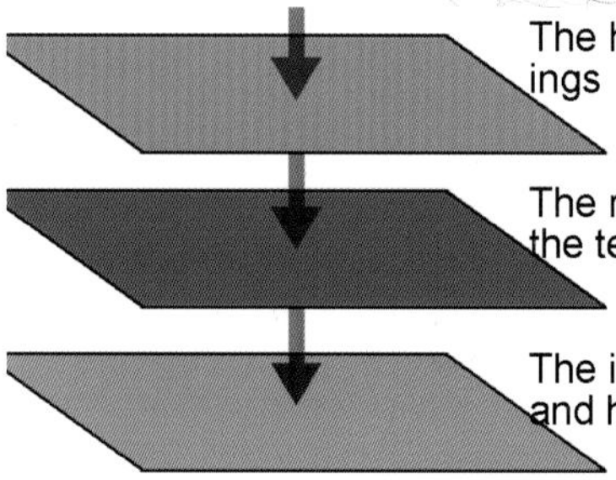

Highest valued

Higly valued

The historical values of the buildings

The religious influential sphere of
the temples/shrines

The integrated map of highest
and highly valued religious build-

3.DESIGN GUIDELINES

Protection
■Any activities leading to the loss
and damage the buildings are prohibited.
■Any activities not compatible with
the activities originally associated
with these buildings are prohibited.

Remedying and Improving:
■Recover the damaged architecture using the traditional techniques and local materials
■Improve the paving using native
materials
■ Increase canopy tree and vegetation to enhance the quality of the
environment
■Add seats, bicycle rental, etc. for
the use of tourists and residents,
which shall not conflict with religious atmosphere
■Add environmental interpretation
to tell the stories of the religious
buildings

*Plate 08 Evaluation and development of design guidelines for spiritual spaces within the village to safeguard the spiritual process of the
local residents.*

1.REPRESENTATION

MAGANG, CHINA

Families and individuals are closely connected in the village through a network of pedestrian streets and lanes. This street network also makes cultural and religious places easily accessible to the villagers.

The most heavily trafficked streets must be kept safe and highly accessible to the community. This will remain important even after the village is integrated into the new urban fabric.

The challenges are:
■Leading the urban development, wide traffic roads are already planned or are under construction,
■The pedestrian streets are also facing the pressure of being widened, which can only be accomplished by taking down the old buildings.
■Traffic roads are also disrupting the connected street network.

The trational steets and lanes

The trational steets and lanes

The trational bridges

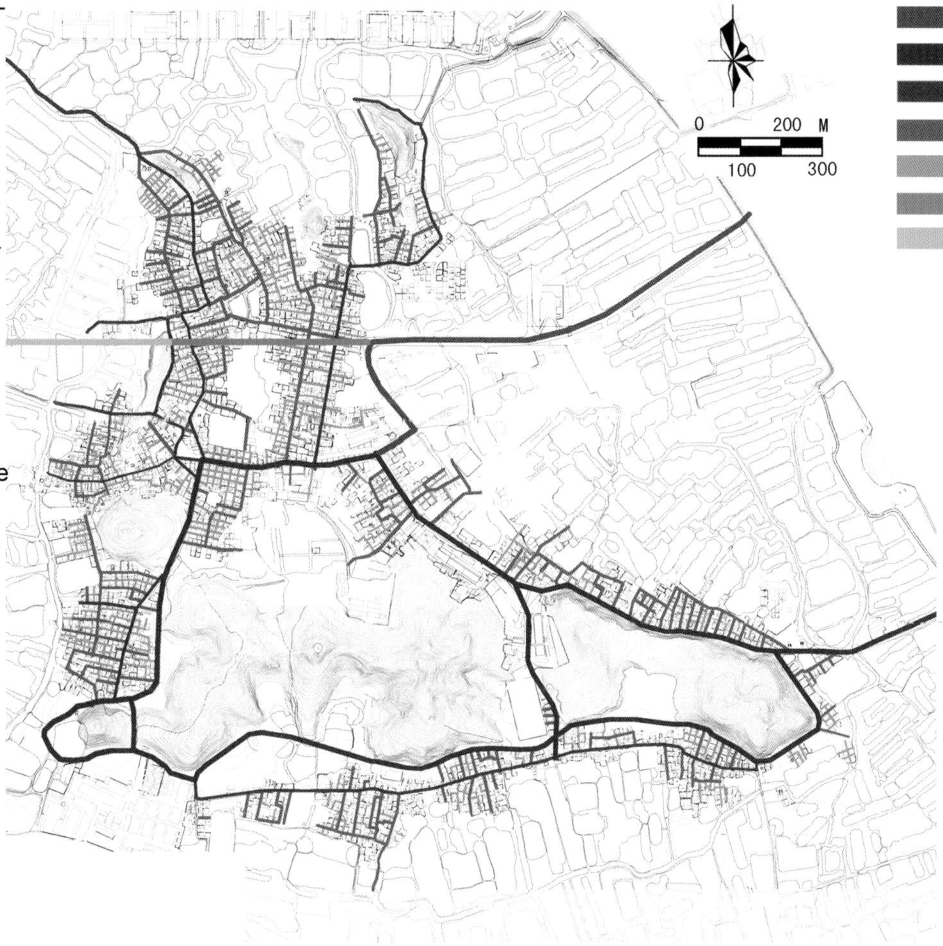

Through traffic road

First-grade village street

Second grade village street

Third-grade village street

Fourth-grade village street

Planned road under construction

Planned road not under construction

0   200 M

100   300

The challenges of urbanization to traditional street system

Plate 09 Street network and connectivity: identification of strategic pedestrian networks within the village.

93

10 STREETS

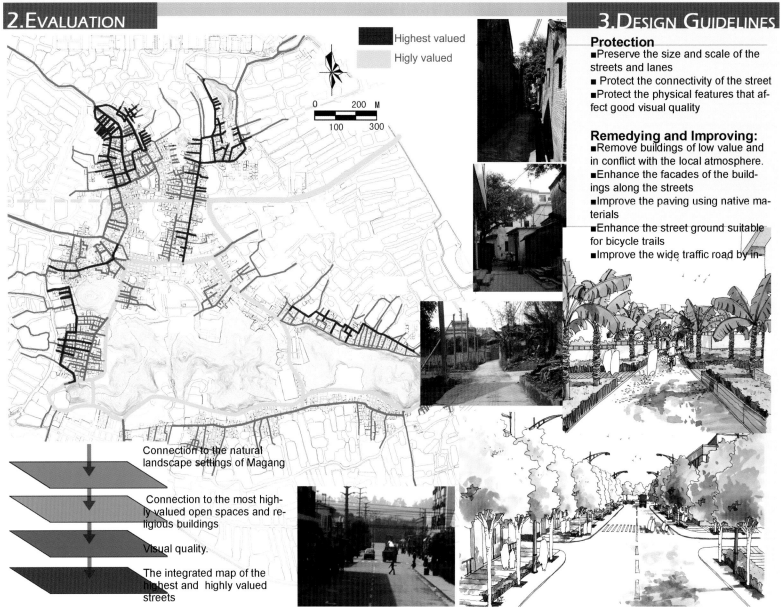

Highest valued

Higly valued

0   200 M

100   300

3. DESIGN GUIDELINES

Protection
■ Preserve the size and scale of the streets and lanes
■ Protect the connectivity of the street
■ Protect the physical features that affect good visual quality

Remedying and Improving:
■ Remove buildings of low value and in conflict with the local atmosphere.
■ Enhance the facades of the buildings along the streets
■ Improve the paving using native materials
■ Enhance the street ground suitable for bicycle trails
■ Improve the wide traffic road by in-

Connection to the natural landscape settings of Magang

Connection to the most highly valued open spaces and religious buildings

Visual quality.

The integrated map of the highest and highly valued streets

Plate 10 Street design ensures connectivity with social processes of the community.

11 RESIDENCE
1. REPRESENTATION

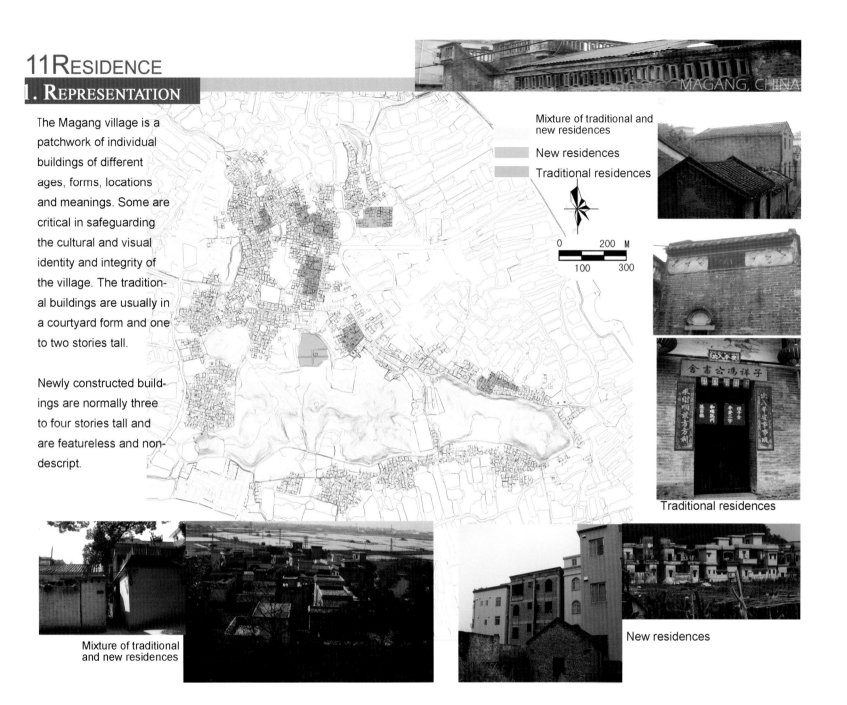

The Magang village is a patchwork of individual buildings of different ages, forms, locations and meanings. Some are critical in safeguarding the cultural and visual identity and integrity of the village. The traditional buildings are usually in a courtyard form and one to two stories tall.

Newly constructed buildings are normally three to four stories tall and are featureless and nondescript.

Mixture of traditional and new residences

New residences

Traditional residences

0   200 M
100   300

Traditional residences

Mixture of traditional and new residences

New residences

Plate 11 Residential and individual buildings add cultural identity.

12 RESIDENCE

2.EVALUATION

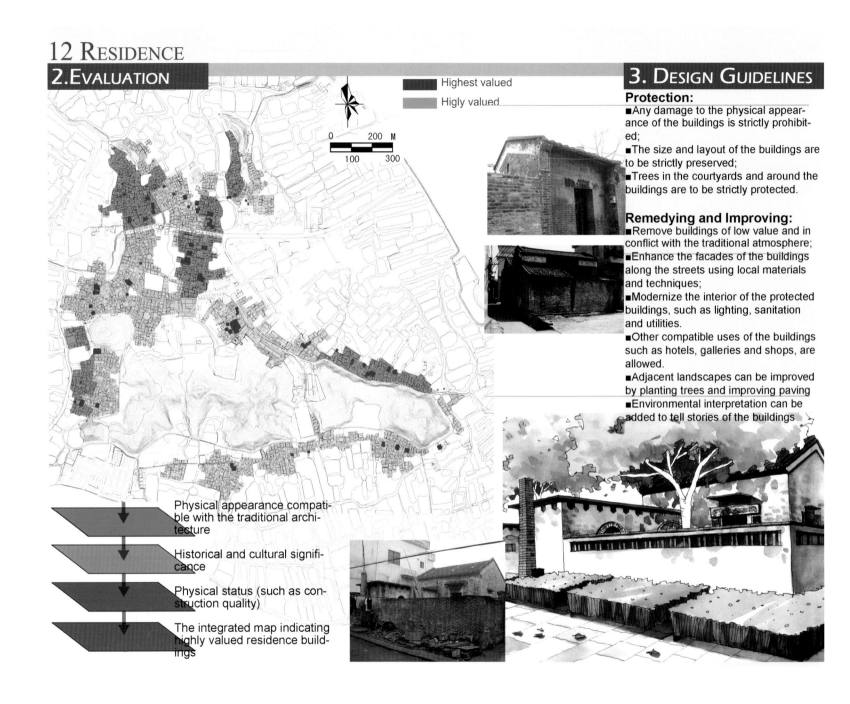

Highest valued

Higly valued

0   200 M

100   300

Physical appearance compatible with the traditional architecture

Historical and cultural significance

Physical status (such as construction quality)

The integrated map indicating highly valued residence buildings

3. DESIGN GUIDELINES

Protection:
■Any damage to the physical appearance of the buildings is strictly prohibited;
■The size and layout of the buildings are to be strictly preserved;
■Trees in the courtyards and around the buildings are to be strictly protected.

Remedying and Improving:
■Remove buildings of low value and in conflict with the traditional atmosphere;
■Enhance the facades of the buildings along the streets using local materials and techniques;
■Modernize the interior of the protected buildings, such as lighting, sanitation and utilities.
■Other compatible uses of the buildings such as hotels, galleries and shops, are allowed.
■Adjacent landscapes can be improved by planting trees and improving paving
■Environmental interpretation can be added to tell stories of the buildings

Plate 12 Residence and individual buildings and cultural identity: evaluate and develop design guidelines for the heritage buildings to safeguard the cultural identity.

13 INTEGRATED STRATEGIC LANDSCAPE PATTERN TO SAFEGUARD MAGAN

1. EVALUATION

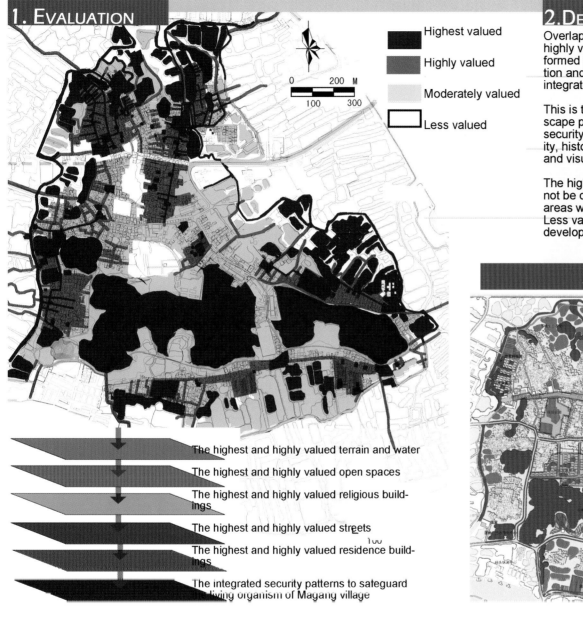

- Highest valued
- Highly valued
- Moderately valued
- Less valued

0   200 M
100   300

The highest and highly valued terrain and water

The highest and highly valued open spaces

The highest and highly valued religious buildings

The highest and highly valued streets

The highest and highly valued residence buildings

The integrated security patterns to safeguard living organism of Magang village

2. DEVELOPMENT GUIDELINES

Overlapping the above five highest and highly valued landscape patterns, which formed the bases for allocation of preservation and new development, has led to the integrated strategic landscape patterns.

This is the most critical and efficient landscape pattern to safeguard the ecological security, spiritual integrity, social connectivity, historical continuity, as well as cultural and visual identity of Magang.

The highest and highly valued areas will not be developed, while moderately valued areas will undergo controlled development. Less valued areas are encouraged for new development

3. DEVELOPABLE AREA

0   200 M
100   300

图 例
可建设区域

Plate 13 The integrated protected strategic landscape patterns to safeguard Magang.

97

14 PLANNING STRATEGIES

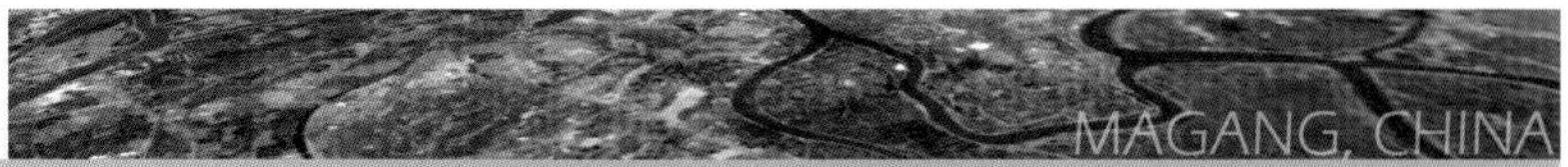

1.NETWORKING

A network of valued and protected cultural landscapes can be built by integrating the critical landscape elements strategically important to safeguarding the ecological, cultural, spiritual and social processes. This landscape network is a minimum baseline for the protection of Magang, which not only ensures the integrity of Magang, but will also act as an experiential route for tourists.

The network is a tie between the history and future, between the old village and the new urban community, between the land and people, and between the native residents and new immigrants. Tourist facilities and environmental information can also be provided along this network.

The network of transportation: traffic is diverted to keep the landscape network safe and pedestrian-friendly.

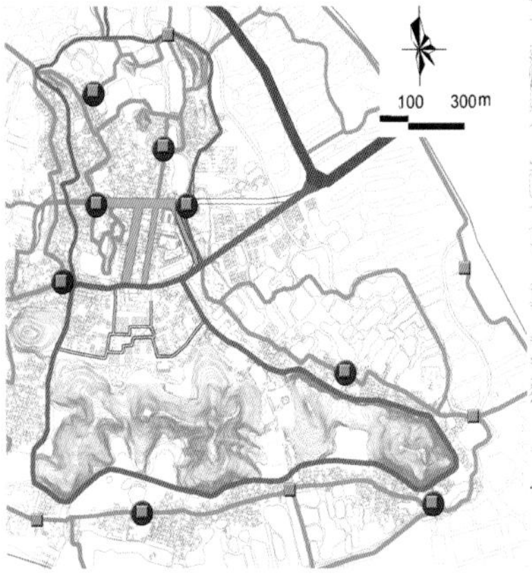

100   300m

Religious festivals

Tea culture display

Local cooking experience
Local foods and art crafts display
Folk art museum

Local handcrafts exhibition

Ancestral temple & family lineage tradition display

Local opera show

Buddha birthday festival

Motor vehicle road
Bicycle route
Pedestrian street and path
● Bus stop
▪ Bicycle rental shop

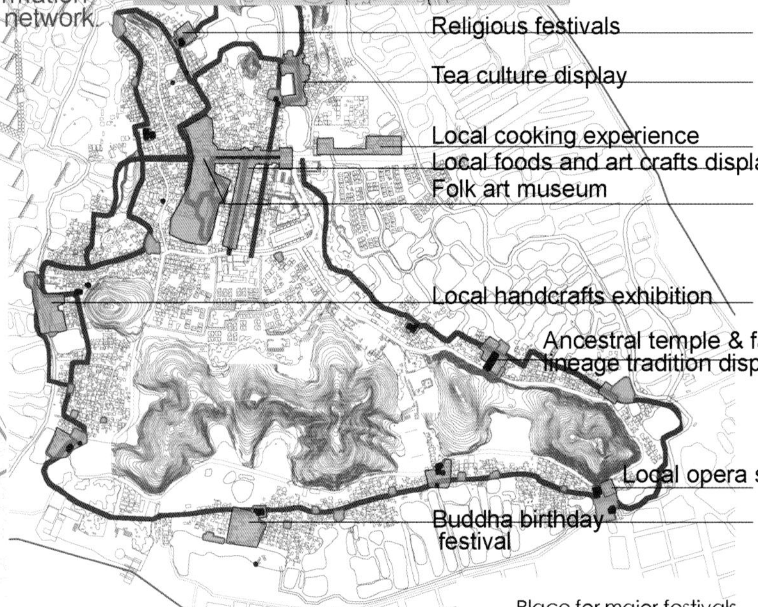

Places for festivals and activities are linked and made easily accessible to tourists and local residents.

Place for major festivals and local activities
Critical open space
Connecting route
■ Religious buildings

Plate 14 Networking of the strategic landscape elements for protection and tourism, allowing the heritage of the existing village to be integrated into the new urban development.

98

15 PLANNING STRATEGIES
2.PATCH WORKIING

As an alternative to the conventional approach of urban development by the total removal of villages, the approach of patching suggests the integration of the existing village landscape with the new development. This interwoven fabric creates social, cultural and spatial diversity, which is the single most important factor to ensuring the vitality of the city.

One section of Magang village, where the indiscriminating development has just gotten underway, is taken as a model for a more detailed design of patch working.

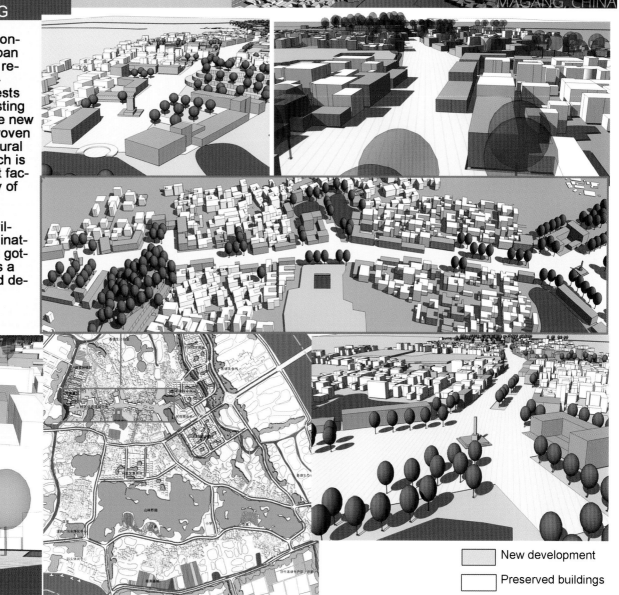

New development

Preserved buildings

Plate 15 The urbanization of the village: one detailed example of the patchwork of the integrated protected buildings and new development along the main street of the village.

The Art of Survival

Survival

Recovering Landscape Architecture

3.1 The Rice Campus: Shenyang Architectural University

The ASLA Design Honor Award, 2005

Kongjian Yu

The Graduate School of Landscape Architecture, Peking University and Turenscape, Beijing, China

1 The Scope and Challenges

In March 2002, the Shenyang City in North China's Liaoning Province commissioned the designer to create a new, 80-hectare suburban campus for Shenyang Architectural University. Originally located downtown, the university was established in 1948 and played an important role in educating architects and civil engineers for the city of Shengyang and for the country as well. But due to a recent dramatic national surge in interest in architecture in China, the enrollment of the school ballooned, creating congestion and overcrowding in its downtown, urban location. After much deliberation, the school decided the best solution was to move the entire campus to the suburbs. The project submitted here is one part of the campus located in the southwest side of the campus, within an area of 3 hectares.

The design team had to contend with the following existing site conditions and budgetary limitations:

1 Former agricultural use: the new site for the proposed campus was originally a rice field, the origin of the famous "Northeast Rice", known for its high quality due to the cool climate, and its longer growing season than rice from southern China (one single crop of rice in this area will last from the mid May till the end of October, while in south China it can only last 100 days. This is one reason that rice can be used as a landscaping material). Soil quality was good and a viable agricultural irrigation system was still in place.

2 Small budget: the budget for landscaping was set at approximately one US dollar per square meter. Most of the budget funded the design and construction of 320,000 square meters in new university buildings.

3 Short timeline: the university required the design to be developed and implemented within one year. Classes were expected to begin in the fall semester of 2003.

2 The Concept

Landscape architects working in China must address issues of food production and sustainable land use, two of the biggest current issues on China's horizon as the country moves toward modernization. The overwhelming urbanization process in China is inevitably encroaching upon a large portion of China's arable lands. With a population of 1.3 billion people, but with only 18 percent arable land, China is in danger of depleting its very valuable and limited resources.

Figure 01a design concept

The concept of this design seeks to use rice, native plants and crops to keep the landscape productive while also fulfilling its new role as an environment for learning.

It is designed to raise awareness of land and farming amongst college students who are leaving the land to become city dwellers. In addition, the designer also seeks to demonstrate how inexpensive and productive agricultural landscape can become, through careful design and management, usable space.

3 The Major Features

1 The productive campus rice paddy: not only designed to be a campus with small open platforms spanning the landscape, the campus is also a completely functional rice paddy, complete with its own system of irrigation.

2 Other native crops, such as buckwheat, grow in annual rotation across the campus. Native plants line pathways.

3 The productive aspect of the landscape draws both students and faculty into the dialogue of sustainable development and food production. By situating a new architecture school within a functioning rice paddy, the design allows the process of agriculture to become transparent and

accessible to all on campus. Management and student participation become part of the productive landscape. The farming processes can potentially become a laboratory for students and the faculty as well.

4 "Golden Rice" became a university icon: the rice produced on the campus is harvested and distributed as Golden Rice, serving both as a keepsake for visitors of the school, and also as a source of identity for the newly established suburban campus. But perhaps most importantly, the widespread distribution of Golden Rice could raise awareness of new hybrid landscape solutions that could both continue old, yet crucial, uses such as food production, while supporting new uses, such as the education of China's new architects.

Project Location: Shenyang City, Liaoning Province, China

Size: 21 hectares

Date of Completion: September, 2003

Owner/Client: Shenyang Architectural University

Design Firm: Turenscape, Beijing, China

Design Principal: Kongjian Yu

Design Team: Long Xiang, Lin Shihong, Han Yi Han, Xiaoye, Zhang Yufei, Zhang Fuchang, Wang Baolin

Photos: Yu, K.J. and Cao, Y.

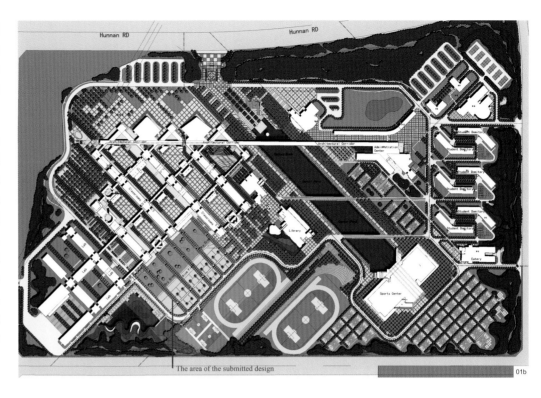

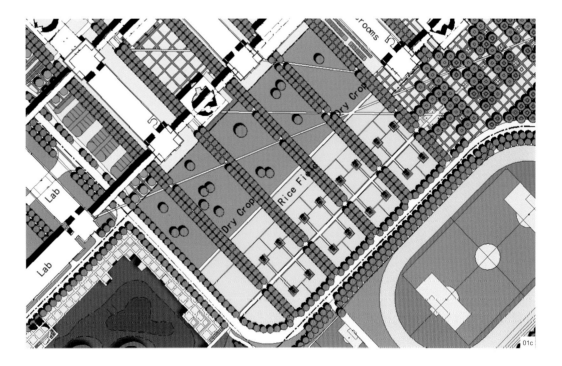

Figure 01b,c Master plan of the campus rice field

103

03a

Figure 02 Aerial view of productive campus: native crops (rice and buckwheat) are used for the new campus landscape. The paths across the field are connections between different functional buildings (between student dormitories to classrooms and laboratories).

Figures 03a,b "Reading in the rice": rice paddies are distributed in combination with elevated study areas; each study area is covered with a native canopy tree.

03b

Figure 04 Professor traveling to classroom.

Figure 05 Leisure time for students.

107

08

Figure 06 Sheep are raised while keeping the native ground cover in shape; native poplar trees are used for shading, and the path is designed for potential mechanical use as well as for daily pedestrian use with a planting band in the center.

Figures 07–09 Rice fields are made penetrable using concrete narrow paths that allow students and faculty staff to touch and feel the rice.

Figure 10 The Rice Planting Day: the first Saturday after mid May was designated as the rice planting day for the university. Students and faculty members will celebrate the planting of rice seedlings. It is an unforgettable and unique experience for the students, and is becoming an integral part of the university culture.

Figure 11 The Rice Harvesting Day: The last Saturday of October each year was designated as the rice harvesting day, when all the students and faculty members participate in harvesting their own rice. This way the long-lost tradition of rice culture in China becomes a campus culture.

Figure 12 Rice paddies were deliberately left on the fields to last until the winter to give a bright and warm color to the cold atmosphere, and also to attract birds to the campus.

Figure 13 The paddies are attractions for birds even in the winter.

Figure 14 "Golden Rice" becomes an icon: the rice produced on the campus is harvested and distributed as Golden Rice, serving both as a keepsake for visitors of the school, and also as a source of identity for the newly established, suburban campus.

15

Figure 15 Rice paddies were deliberately left on the fields to last until the winter, giving a bright and warm color to the cold atmosphere, and also attracting birds to the campus.

Figures 16a,b The harvested rice is packed for drying, creating another unique landscape in the campus.

Figures 17a,b The Campus is a favorable site for tourism and education.

Figure 18 Native plants (Polygonum) covering the slopes of the university sports field and rice paddies.

3.2 The Floating Gardens: The Yongning River Park

The China Human Habitat Award, 2005

The ASLA Design Honor Award, 2006

Kongjian Yu

The Graduate School of Landscape Architecture, Peking University and Turenscape, Beijing, China

In July 2002, Taizhou City invited the landscape architecture company, Turenscape, to design a 21-hectare park along the Yongning River, the mother river of the historical city on the east coast of China. At that time, the site along the river had concrete banks that were part of the local government's flood control policy.

The design objective for this park included an overall concept that would create accessibility for both tourists and locals. Another key objective was to provide an alternative flood control and storm water management solution to be used as a model for the entire river valley.

The result was the Floating Gardens.

1 Challenges Faced by the Landscape Architect

1 The local authority's practice was to realign and channel the river with concrete embankments. This common engineering solution is ecologically destructive to the inter-tidal zones and river morphology; and also culturally and historically insensitive to local traditions that the river symbolizes to the local inhabitants. Additionally, this type of practice is an economically irresponsible way to use valuable public funds, due to its high costs relative to other public projects.

2 To design an alternative flood control and storm water management solution as a model for the entire river valley. Most rivers in China share the same fate because of the country's rapid urbanization; flood-control projects based on outdated and un-ecological engineering practices. As a model for the Yongning River, this project has the potential to be a national infrastructure model for all riverfront design and flood-control projects in China.

3 To design a park that serves multiple purposes: ecological river habitats allow natural tidal fluctuations, and are still accessible for tourists and the local community.

2 Design Solutions: The Floating Gardens

The concept of Floating Gardens was developed to meet the challenges listed above.

The park is composed of two layers: the natural matrix overlapped with the human matrix—the floating gardens. The natural matrix is composed of wetland and natural vegetation designed for the natural processes of flooding and native habitats. Above this natural matrix, "float" the gardens that serve humanity. This is composed of a system that includes: a tree matrix, a circulation path network, and a matrix of story boxes.

The design draws on the following aspects:

1 A regional drainage approach that takes into account the storm water process analysis for flood patterns at every 5-, 20-, and 50-year levels. These analyses became the basis for the park's design.

2 An alternative flood control solution that utilizes constructed wetlands that are based on incorporating the regional flood patterns into the overall park design. The site along the river is intended to be a multifunctional project.

3 The matrix layer for the natural processes is composed of a restored riparian wetland along the flood plain and an outer wetland (lake) outside the riverbank and runs parallel to the river for the length of the park boundary. The park design utilizes native plant communities and takes into account the monsoon season and its flooding habits. During the dry season, the design of the outer wetland plant communities incorporates fresh water from the inlet located in the upper reach of the river. Year round, the water is accessible to park users.

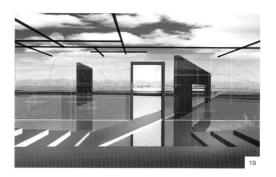

4 Masses of native wetland plants, trees, and bamboos are introduced along the riverbank as a method to promote continuity of the design with the surrounding ecosystem.

5 The upper layer for humanity that "floats" above the seasonally flooded natural matrix is composed of a complex of groves of native trees interwoven with a path network that extends from the urban fabric. A system of story boxes is strategically located along the path and is intended to create a local folk narrative including: a box of rice, a box of fish, a box of hardware crafts, a box of Taoism, a box of stone, a box of mountain and water, a box of citrus, and a box of martial arts. The use of boxes is a design method that frames scenes with special themes that occur visually within a large landscape background.

3 The Significance of the Park

The design is an innovative approach that is ecologically sensitive to understanding the river's dynamic flows and tides. The park design is also intended to educate park users and demonstrate alternative solutions to flood-control engineering and water management.

Floating Gardens utilizes design techniques that appear simplistic to create an accessible and interesting landscape dominated by nature.

Project Location: Taizhou City, Zhejiang Province, China

Size: 21.3 hectares

Date of Completion: March, 2004

Owner/Client: The Government of Huanyan District, Taizhou City

Design Firm: Turenscape, Beijing, China

Design Principal: Kongjian YU

Design Team: Liu Yujie, Liu Dongyun, Lin Shihong, Jin Yuanyuan, Zheng Gang, Liang Tailong, Ning Weijiing, Ge Mingyu

Photos: Yu, K.J. and Cao, Y.

Figure 20 View of the site before park construction: the riverbank was lined with concrete and the artificial process of canalization was underway.

Figure 21 The park during construction: concrete embankment was removed; diverse terrain on the river bed and along the riparian plane were introduced to create a variety of native plant communities and related animal habitats. The river bank was re-articulated to allow the public access to the water.

Figure 22 The ecologically recovered riparian wetland is conducive to the natural processes of flooding; native species are also accessible to people.

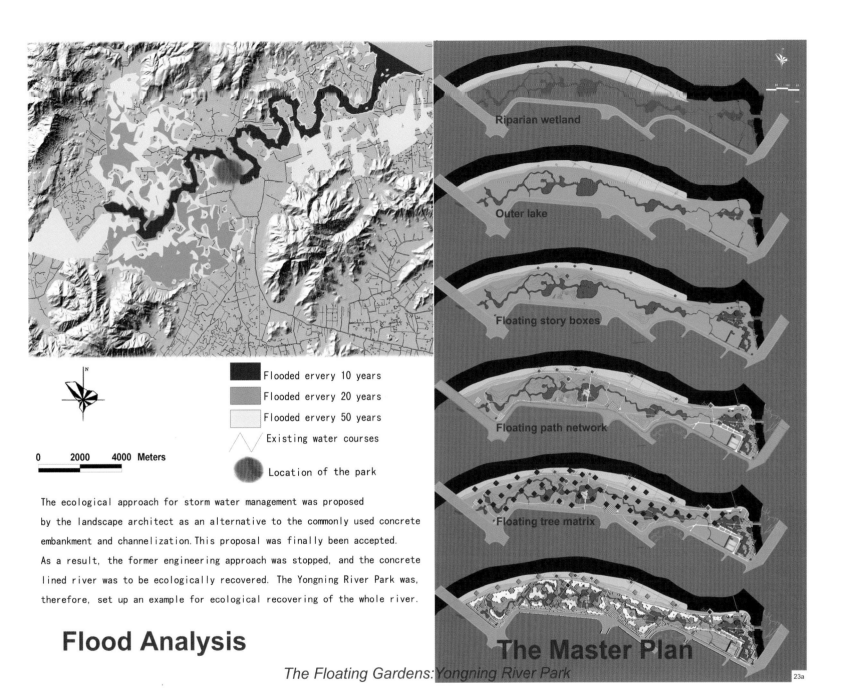

Flooded ervery 10 years
Flooded ervery 20 years
Flooded ervery 50 years
Existing water courses
Location of the park

0   2000   4000   Meters

The ecological approach for storm water management was proposed
by the landscape architect as an alternative to the commonly used concrete
embankment and channelization. This proposal was finally been accepted.
As a result, the former engineering approach was stopped, and the concrete
lined river was to be ecologically recovered. The Yongning River Park was,
therefore, set up an example for ecological recovering of the whole river.

Flood Analysis

Riparian wetland

Outer lake

Floating story boxes

Floating path network

Floating tree matrix

The Master Plan

The Floating Gardens: Yongning River Park

23a

Figure 23a,b The master plan and the potential flooding pattern of the drainage basin provide an ecologically sound alternative solution for storm water management. A wetland system both inside and outside of the riparian plane was introduced. This natural landscape becomes the background where the gardens of human elements can float.

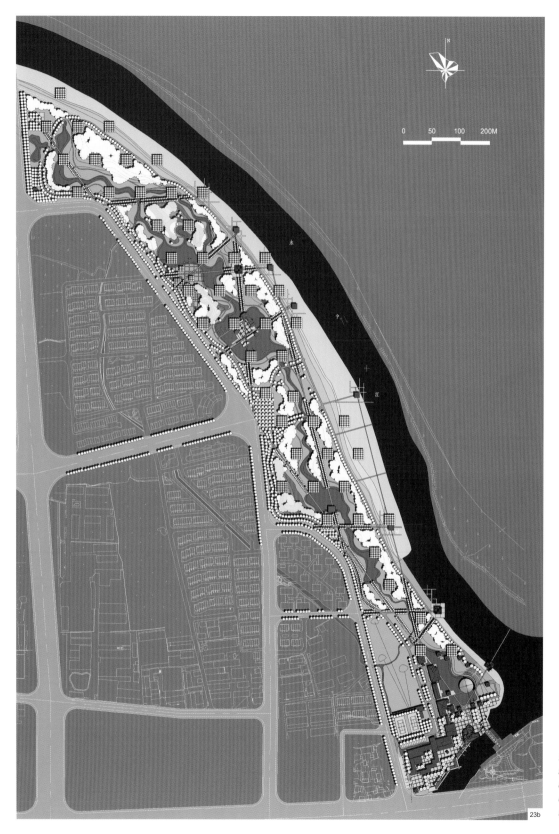

23b

Figure 24 The ecologically recovered riparian wetland is conducive to the natural processes of flooding and provides access to native plant species.

24

25a

Figures 25a,b, 26 Native grasses were used to consolidate the riverbank and to create an attractive setting for visitors.

Figure 27 An environmental installation of columns tells the story of martial art (gong fu), for which the town Huangyan is famous. The columns allow water to drain during the flooding season and create a lively atmosphere for visitors to enjoy.

25b

26

Figure 28 A strong contrast exists between the native grasses and designed artwork installed on the riparian plane.

Figures 29a,b A floating box above the riparian wetland: one of the eight-story boxes that use a minimum formalistic geometry and spatial language to create a narrative for the local cultural heritage.

Figure 30a–c The native grass in front of simple and pure story boxes.

29a

29b

127

30a

30b

30c

Figure 31 Story box of stone displays the unique rock found in region: the yellow rock, for which Huangyan town was named. The yellow box sets up a frame to display this common local rock, making it both special and memorable.

Figure 32 The manmade wetland (lake) outside the riverbank runs parallel to the river. A network of bridges and paths is overlaid with a series of story boxes.

34

Figure 34 A teahouse in the park is sited harmoniously within the surrounding natural setting.

Figure 35 One of the lanes that creates the path network is lined with bamboo. The landscape architect allows common material to appear fresh and innovative.

35

135

The Art of Survival

Recovering Landscape Architecture

4.1 Zhongshan Shipyard Park

The ASLA Design Honor Award, 2002

The China National Architectural Art Award, 2004

The Gold Medal of Fine Art, China, 2004

Kongjian Yu and Wei Pang

The Graduate School of Landscape Architecture, Peking University and Turenscape, Beijing, China

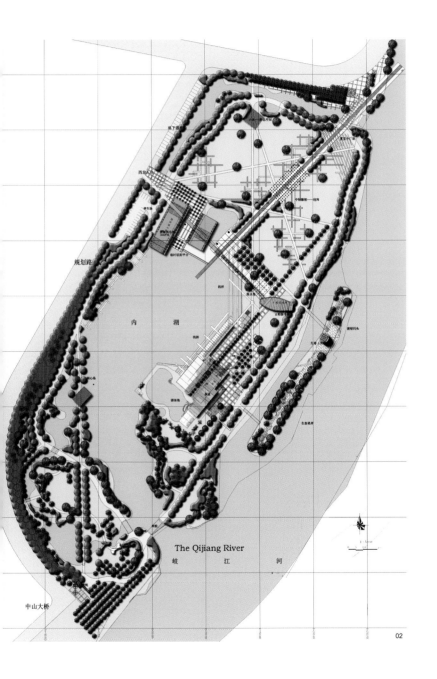

The Qijiang River

02

Figure 01 Overview

Figure 02 Master plan

Figure 03 Aerial view of the park

03

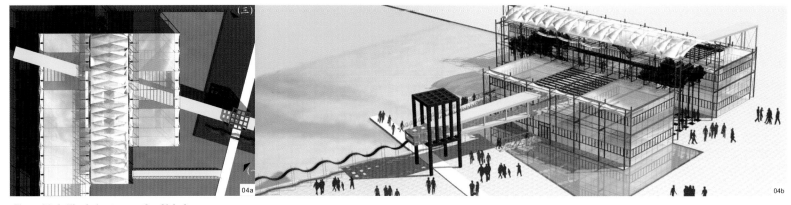

Figure 04a,b The design to reuse the old docks

This park was built on an old shipyard site and dirt field. The design is a model for landscape architects in China. It demonstrates how to transform a derelict industrial site into a beautiful, meaningful, and functional place. It also represents an emerging role for landscape architects in urban renovation projects.

The following aspects of this project make it unique:

1 Its Unique History: a Small Site with Big Stories

The shipyard was originally built in the 1950s and went bankrupt in 1999. Though small in scale, it reflects the remarkable 50-year history of socialist China, including the cultural revolution of the 1960s and 70s. As such, the site has many memories and provides opportunities to tell stories to those who did not experience this historical period.

2 A Challenging Setting: Water Level Fluctuations, Tree Preservation, and Design with Machines

The site's inventory of existing features includes: remnants and machinery of the shipyard, lake with fluctuating water levels from sea influences, and mature trees and vegetation. These provided design challenges as follows:

Challenge 1 Fluctuating water levels: with the existing lake connected to the Qijiang River and sea, water levels fluctuate up to 1.1 meters daily. To deal with this challenge, a network of bridges was constructed at various elevations. Terraced planting beds were integrated with this network to allow public access to the native weeds. As a result, visitors can feel the ocean breeze.

Challenge 2 Balance river width regulations for flood control while protecting old fichus trees along the riverbank. Regulations of the Water Management Bureau required the river corridor at the east side of the site to be expanded from 60 meters to 80 meters. This was a water management requirement and meant that a stand of mature banyan trees was at risk of destruction. The approach was to dig a parallel 20-meter-wide ditch on each side of the linear stand of trees. This resulted in the creation of an island that preserved the stand of mature banyan trees, a significant preservation effort.

Challenge 3 Remnant rust docks and machinery—nothing as gigantic or unusual as a gasworks or steel factory. As purely preserved elements, the former shipyard machinery might become a distraction or nuisance for local residents. Three approaches are taken to artistically and ecologically capture the spirit of the site using these elements: preservation, modification of old forms, and creation of new forms. New forms include a network of straight paths, a red box and a green box that dramatize the character of the site in an artistic way.

The design intentions are as follows

1 Site Opportunities and Detailed Design

Preservation and adaptive reuse measures were taken. Efforts were taken to preserve vegetation along the lakeshore as well as retaining all heritage trees. Reusing existing materials and machinery was also included in the design approach. A careful detailed inventory of existing materials provided the basis for the detailed design and Turenscape's design intentions.

2 Functionalism

Program and function is a key driving force for the project design. A network of pedestrian paths link various park features: important locations and exits, tea houses and club houses that are created from existing docks, the accessible terraced native planting areas, the new light tower created from the former water tower, and the paved areas under trees for shadow boxing.

3 Relationship to the Urban Context

The park merges into the urban fabric by extending the adjacent circulation flow into the park's circulation network. Urban recreational facilities like a teahouse and museum are provided in the park. The tradition in the area includes a daily lifestyle that involves drinking tea in teahouses.

4 Environmental Responsibility

The principle of reducing, reusing, and recycling natural and manmade materials is carried out throughout project. Original vegetation, soil, and natural habitats were preserved. To supplement this local ecology, native plant materials were used throughout the park. Machines, docks and other structures were reused for educational, aesthetic, and functional purposes.

Project Location: Zhongshan City, Guangdong Province, China

Size: 11 hectares

Date of Completion: May, 2001

Owner/Client: Government of Zhongshan City

Design Firm: Turenscape, Beijing, China

Design Principal: Kongjian Yu

Design Team: Kongjian Yu, Pang Wei, Huang Zhengzheng, Qiu Qingyuan, Lin Shihong Lin

Photography: Yu, K.J. and Cao, Y.

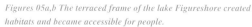

Figures 05a,b The terraced frame of the lake Figureshore created habitats and became accessible for people.

05a

05b

Figures 06a-d The reuse of docks for various functions including new boating facilities and art museum.

Figures 07a,b Rails were preserved and reused.

06a

06c

06b

06d

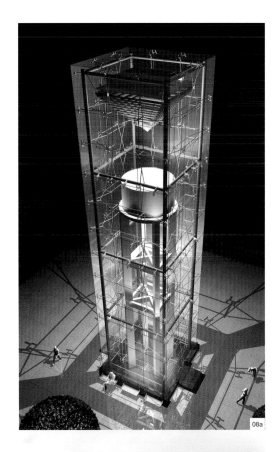

Figures 08a–d Two water towers were reused and redesigned.

09a

Figure 09a,b Machinery and artifacts were reused and recycled.

10a

Figure 10a,b Native grasses were used widely in the park.

10b

11

12a

Figure 11 New design: new bridge crosses the lake.
Figures 12a–f New design: red box and red memory.

4.1a Industrial Strength: Zhongshan Shipyard Park

At a former shipyard, a park design breaks with convention to honor China's recent past

Mary G. Padua

University of Hong Kong Faculty of Architecture

During the past half century, China has lived through a period of extraordinary change. In just over 50 years, the country has been transformed from a semi-feudal society dominated by foreign interests, to an economic superpower exerting claims to authority in the world. The nation has lived through revolution, famine, waves of massive centralization and decentralization, isolationism, and entry into the World Trade Organization. The Chinese record of lifting people out of extreme poverty is unequaled in world history.

This dizzying history has created major social discontinuities. The misery of periods like Mao Tse-Tung's "Great Leap Forward", in which millions starved, and violent episodes like the Cultural Revolution and Tiananmen Square have left the Chinese people with historical blind spots. Although these events are within the personal experience of many, there is a collective effort to banish them from memory. The result is a cultural personality split. People are enamored with things that are modern and international, and they show great respect for elements that are seen as classically Chinese, but much of 20th-century Chinese history has become forbidden territory.

This atmosphere poses particular challenges for landscape architects. A designer can appropriate elements of classical Chinese gardens and assemble them into landscapes that resemble the popular image of a traditional design. Or a designer can transpose elements from projects in other parts of the world and provide a completely contemporary solution. Either approach might satisfy the client, but the resulting design solution is divorced from context and offers little more than decorative content.

When seen in the light of these conventions, the award-winning Zhongshan Shipyard Park is a ground-breaking project for contemporary Chinese landscape architecture. Professor Kongjian Yu and his team from Turenscape took the risk of rejecting popular attitudes toward design and created a new approach that acknowledges and incorporates the recent past. The 25-acre park combines historical, contemporary, and ecological elements in a place that is both a living memorial to China's recent past and a vibrant part of everyday life in the southern Chinese city of Zhongshan.

As its name implies, the park was created on the site of a former shipyard. Zhongshan is located in Guangdong Province, which lies along the South China Sea and shares a border with Hong Kong. The heart of Guangdong Province is the Pearl River Delta. The delta, traditionally a rich agricultural region, is now also home to the largest concentration of manufacturing industries in China. Zhongshan lies in the western part of the region, 86 kilometers south of the provincial capital Guangzhou (formerly Canton). Zhongshan's location on a tributary of the Pearl River made it a natural site for shipbuilding, and the Yuezhong Shipyard was the industrial heart of the city for nearly half a century. At one time, the shipyard was the largest employer in Zhongshan—housing, feeding, and caring for 1300 workers on the shipyard site.

Zhongshan Shipyard Park was designed as a tribute to the shipyard workers and millions of others who helped to build modern Chinese society. However, there is nothing nostalgic or traditional about the park design. Yu and his team incorporated design elements unknown in traditional Chinese parks and broke with prevailing practice by recycling industrial buildings and other remnants of the old shipyard.

The process involved major challenges for Turenscape. The design had to preserve natural habitats while responding to environmental problems that required major alterations in the riverfront along one edge of the park. At the same time, Turenscape had to deal with a governmental design–review committee that had difficulty understanding and accepting the firm's unorthodox approach to the social and cultural aspects of site.

Zhongshan Shipyard Park today is a dramatic melding of local history and the natural environment that has become an integral part of the city's urban fabric. The park offers people a rich variety of experiences. Children and adults play in its fountains, stream, and lake. Elderly people do their morning tai chi exercises on the lawns and plazas. Former shipyard workers relive memories, and students contemplate a history that they know only from books.

I visited the park four times in the course of three days in February. My initial encounter with the park took place under ideal conditions: a sunny, warm Saturday afternoon, the last day of the Chinese lunar New Year celebration. Yu and Pang Wei, from Turenscape, met me at the park for a personal tour.

The first thing most visitors see is the main entry, a granite plaza organized around a fountain built of steel plates with notional rivers intended to evoke large steel trusses used in bridge and factory construction. The plates extend into the adjacent paving, creating continuity with the larger plaza area. Bubble jets are located in the spaces created by intersections of the steel plates. Adults and children were playing together in the fountain when we arrived, giving the plaza a warm, welcoming feeling despite the industrial character of the design.

An artificial stream separates the plaza from the park. The stream provides another place for people to play, masks noise from the adjacent roadway, and creates a transition from the surrounding urban context. Its picturesque effect recalls the use of water in classic Chinese scholar gardens, where quiet pools and streams reflect the surroundings and promote contemplation.

Boulders are placed at key points in the stream to create bridges to the path system of the park. While people do climb over these informal

bridges to get into the park, most visitors enter on a broad, paved path past a stand of bamboo at the edge of a tile stream. The bamboo marks the park entrance and is a reference to traditional Chinese gardens where bamboo symbolizes nobility.

The use of design elements that have multiple meanings is central to Yu's approach. Features throughout the park combine recreational uses with symbolic references to the history of the site and modern China. Yu is deeply aware of the hardships and labor that went into building the society, and he has attempted to infuse the park with that awareness.

The railroad path, a striking 3-meter-wide walkway, stretches a half-mile from the main entry to the lakefront. Rails and ties laid in the center of the path are highlighted by a bed of white rocks bordered by native grasses and granite walks. The path is the major organizing axis of the park, and it evokes the rails used to move vessels in and out of the water in the shipyard. Children enjoy balancing on the rails while their parents watch from nearby granite walks.

Turenscape's original concept for the railroad path was a broad, straight walkway with strong industrial references that symbolize economic progress in modern China. Members of the local review panel felt that an axial path of this type lacked a sense of climax or focus, and they insisted on placing a grid of 180 slender, white columns at the center point of the railroad path. The columns do focus attention—particularly when uplighted at night—but they are not well integrated into the park design. The grid has a monumental feel more in keeping with 1950's socialist architecture and it lacks any obvious symbolic or historical references.

Not all of the symbolism in the park emphasizes progress in China. The feature that leaves the strongest impression on most visitors is the Red Box, which Yu designed as a room for contemplation of the Cultural Revolution—one of the grimmest periods of recent Chinese history. It is a construction of red-painted steel plates, 9 meters square and about 3 meters high that encloses reflecting pools. An adjacent marker calls attention to the profound political implications of the color red in China and reminds visitors of some of the famous sayings of Lenin and Mao. The symbolism may seem heavy-handed to an outsider, but it carries a great deal of weight in a country whose national anthem remains "The East Is Red". The Red Box seems to touch everyone who visits it: couples pause to embrace inside the space, children run their hands through the water, and elderly people stand and think quietly.

The Green Rooms are another impressive and somewhat unsettling feature of the park. They are areas of about 16 square feet enclosed in 8-foot vertical hedges and carpeted in lawn, and they provide intimate spaces for reading and relaxation. They are very popular, particularly with young couples looking for privacy. More than two dozen Green Rooms are scattered in the areas around the lake.

The intimacy of the Green Rooms also has a disturbing side. Yu designed each room to the dimensions of a workers' dormitory in the old Yuezhong Shipyard. The realization that a dozen workers might have lived for 20 years in a concrete room of this size offers a striking contrast between past and present and a powerful reminder of recent Chinese history.

The lakefront offers a different type of experience. The lake, which is connected to the

Qijiang River, is subject to daily tidal fluctuations of about 1 meter. This created a serious problem for Turenscape designers, who wanted to create access to the lakefront regardless of tidal conditions. They met this challenge with a set of bridges that allow lakefront access at all times of the day. The bridges serve as platforms for viewing the rich array of native plants that Turenscape placed along the shoreline. The shoreline also features two pavilions adapted from old shipyard buildings. The buildings were stripped to structural skeletons, reinforced, and repainted. One now is a red steel skeleton, and the other is white reinforced concrete. The view from inside the pavilions is a framed image of the lake that conveys a strong sense of stillness and tranquility.

Many other structures and pieces of equipment from the shipyard also were recycled in the parks. A pair of huge cranes, originally used to move ships, are a good example. They have been incorporated into gateways on the western and southern edges of the park. The southern gateway combines one of the cranes with park service buildings, and the western gateway joins the other crane to a human-scale sculpture of two shipyard workers. The sculpture is a popular attraction, and visitors come to the gateway to pose with the figures in playful ways.

Turenscape also used sculpture to transform a notoriously troublesome industrial chimney into an installation piece. Steel scaffolding and bronze figures of workers were added to the chimney to create a memorial to the unknown people who labored to keep the shipyard running for half a century.

In some cases, Turenscape built symbolic representations of shipyard structures that had become unsalvageable. A water tower to be reused in the park turned out to be unusable, and Turenscape created a new construction mimicking the skeleton of the original tower. The result is a striking, red steel structure that is positioned to create a sight line along one of the paths leading out of the Red Box. Turenscape followed a similar concept in creating a new museum in the image of an old factory building. Although the original building is gone, Turenscape has recycled its image in the museum and gallery.

The biggest piece of construction in the park is an "ecological island" (as it is called in Chinese) created to save a stand of heritage banyan trees. The trees were on the riverbank that forms the eastern boundary of the park. Flooding is a major problem during the summer monsoons in southern China, and there were plans to widen the river and eliminate the trees. Turenscape solved the problem by creating an island in the river separated from the park by a flood-control channel. A lighthouse on the island—created from another old water tower—is visible for several miles and helps to make the park a local landmark.

Many features of the park, such as the ecological island, the redesigned lakefront, and the native plants, would be modest efforts toward environmentally sensitive design by North American and European standards, but they represent significant advances in Chinese park design. Ecological design is in its infancy in China, where even basic ideas like using local native plants are unknown to most park designers. One of Yu's objectives was to educate the public about these issues and increase local awareness of the region's rich agricultural heritage.

Most Chinese parks are fenced and require an admission fee, but Zhongshan Shipyard Park is free of charge and heavily visited by young and old. People in China sometimes say that the ultimate measure of a park is whether couples use the setting for their wedding photographs. On our last Sunday afternoon, a man and wife in wedding dress were posed by the lakeside pavilion, creating their own memorial to a piece of Chinese history.

The park concept originated in the late 1990s with the deputy mayor of Zhongshan, Peng Jiangwen. After operating for nearly 50 years, the Yuezhong Shipyard was slated to close in 1998. City administrators were attempting to revitalize the downtown area to attract foreign investment, and Peng understood that open space can stimulate property development and tourism. Peng had met Yu at a conference in Beijing, and he decided to contact Turenscape for help. Zhongshan Shipyard Park became a collaboration between the mayor, other city officials, and Turenscape.

Turenscape is one of the largest landscape architecture firms in China, with 150 employees drawn from backgrounds in architecture, planning, and landscape architecture. The firm's approach is interdisciplinary, and its scope of services covers landscape architecture, urban design, architecture, environmental design, community planning, and ecological planning and design. Yu received his bachelor's and master's degrees in landscape architecture from Beijing Forestry University and a Doctor of Design (D.Des) degree from Harvard. He currently teaches at Beijing University, where he is involved in establishing a new graduate school of landscape architecture. The objective of the new program is to upgrade landscape architecture education in China from its traditional status as a branch of agricultural science largely devoted to landscape gardening.

Yu is a native of sortheast China, so his first task in the design process was to learn about the history of the site and southern China. He found Zhongshan and the Yuezhong Shipyard to be emblematic of the 20th-century history of the region and the nation. Zhongshan takes its name from its most prominent native, Sun Yat-sen, who is celebrated as the leader of the original revolutionary movement of the 1920s (the name "Zhongshan" is a Mandarin Chinese equivalent of the Cantonese name "Yatsen"). This link to Sun Yat-sen is cherished by the population of southern China, and it is an important element of the identity of the city.

Since the days of Sun Yat-sen, the area has undergone two major transitions: from traditional agriculture to heavy industry and from heavy industry to modern manufacturing. The shipyard was the core of Zhongshan's industry throughout a large part of this period, operating continuously through the Great Leap Forward of the 1950s, the upheavals of the Cultural Revolution in the 1960s, Deng Xiaoping's reforms in the 1970s, and the rapid growth of export manufacturing in the 1980s and 1990s. By the late 1990s, the local economy had shifted to producing electronics, and the shipyard became obsolete.

When it was operating, the Yuezhong Shipyard was much more than just an employer to the people of Zhongshan. State-owned enterprises like Yuezhong were one of the foundations of the communist society envisioned by Mao, and they became monolithic social institutions that encompassed all aspects of the lives of their employees. Workers lived in dormitories on the shipyard site, they ate in canteens on site, their children were educated in schools run by the shipyard, and they received their medical care in clinics provided by the shipyard.

Yu felt it was vital for the design to preserve continuity with this history, but he did not want to create a park divorced from the contemporary urban fabric of Zhongshan or the modern life of the region and nation. In the social climate of the late 1990s, the comfortable route for Turenscape would have been to design a park that concealed the site's history behind a facade of traditional elements. Instead, Yu chose an approach that encourages contemplation of recent history without glorifying it or denying it.

At the same time, the Zhongshan city administrators wanted a design sensitive to the natural environment of the site. They recognized that serious environmental degradation has taken place in the region during the last few decades, and they are working to strike a balance between promoting industry and creating a habitable city. Their efforts helped Zhongshan to be designated a Chinese National Garden City and to be awarded the prestigious United Nations Habitat Scroll of Honour for improvement of the urban environment.

Turenscape faced a number of major challenges at the site. In addition to the problems posed by the natural environment, the designers had to deal with badly deteriorated structures and machinery scattered throughout the area. Preservation of the site's historical identity ruled out clearing it, but the abandoned items created major aesthetic and environmental problems. However, some local officials did not appreciate the symbolic significance of these objects and were eager to sell them as scrap. In response to these challenges, Yu formulated three major objectives:

To create a park that is part of the urban fabric, accessible to local people and attractive to tourists; to promote recognition of the history of the site and the larger history of China during the

twentieth century; and to preserve any existing ecological value of the site and increase awareness of the rich agricultural heritage of the region. The design review process proved to be demanding and unusual for China. Municipal decision making in China typically resides with a few officials, and design review is carried out with little participation by the general public. By contrast, the approach adopted by the Zhongshan city administration and Turenscape involved extensive public review and participation.

This approach was partially a strategic move by city officials. Deputy Mayor Peng recognized that Turenscape's design was likely to be controversial, and the public review process offered an opportunity to obtain input from future users of the park and build support for the proposal. The strong local attachment to the memory and ideals of Sun Yat-sen also made it easier to undertake a process of this type in Zhongshan; officials like the deputy mayor could call upon a tradition of political openness that helped to give legitimacy to the approach and encourage participation.

The process lasted a year and a half. It was led by Zhongshan officials with the assistance of Turenscape. Turenscape presented the plan to community groups, broadcast additional presentations on cable television, and displayed models and plans in public buildings. Although participation was limited by North American standards, it was unparalleled in China.

The public received the plan warmly, and former shipyard employees and their families were particularly pleased. However, the local government review panel, which included representatives from public bureaus and design faculty from universities in the area, was less enthusiastic. The panel questioned the purpose of reusing machinery from, the old shipyard and failed to see the point of specifying local plants, which they saw as generally unkempt and lacking ornamental value. Objections also were mounted to the rectilinear path system proposed for the park. Typical Chinese park design still follows the model of the Scholar Gardens, in which curving paths symbolize nature. Some panel members saw the straight paths of the Turenscape design as a violation of Chinese garden tradition.

Yu worked with members of the review panel to help them understand the design. He showed images of Richard Haag's Gasworks Park in Seattle and Peter Latz's Duisburg-Nord Landscape Park in Duisburg, Germany, and helped to educate the panel in the changing aesthetics of contemporary landscape design. Yu and his team also spent time explaining how old structures and mechanisms retained in the site could be made safe for the general public. After a lengthy review of plans and sketches, Turenscape prevailed. The panel introduced some significant design alterations, but the master plan for the park remained substantially intact.

The complexity of the design and limitations of local construction expertise made it necessary for Turenscape to collaborate with the Zhongshan Construction Bureau in building the park. Because political pressures dictated completion within a single year, Turenscape and the Zhongshan Construction Bureau adopted a design/build approach, often going straight from original sketches and plans to the field. Yu and his team oversaw the construction process and sometimes participated in construction tasks. Their involvement allowed Turenscape to exert a high level of control over quality and facilitated on-site experimentation with details. The resulting park stands out in China for its standard of construction and quality of detail. Contemporary Chinese parks rarely achieve world construction standards, but Zhongshan Shipyard Park is comparable to high-profile projects in Europe, North America, or Japan.

"A small park that tells a big story" is Yu's description of the project. The story it tells is about 50 years of collective struggle to build a new Chinese society. It is also a story about changes in China today, as a new generation of landscape architects takes on experiments like the Zhongshan Shipyard Park.

The city of Zhongshan and Turenscape stepped off safe territory when they committed to this design. The commitment is a major one in financial and practical terms—the park cost 50 million yuan for an area of 10 hectares. Even more important, it is a commitment to the creation of a new design vocabulary for China. This vocabulary incorporates ideas from across the globe, but it is profoundly Chinese in language and meaning.

Park design has been evolving rapidly during the last two decades. Parks like Duisburg-Nord or Parc de la Villette in France offer new models and have helped to pioneer new styles. Zhongshan Shipyard Park may offer a similar model for China in the 21st century—an approach to design that is open to the world, unflinching in its view of recent history, and fundamentally Chinese.

PROJECT CREDITS

Designers: Turenscape and the Center for Landscape Architecture, Beijing University. Kongjian Yu, ASLA, project director and principal designer

Turenscape landscape architects: Pang Wei, Huang Zhengzheng, Li Jiang-hong, Lin Shihong, Li Xianghua, Zhang Juang, Hu Haibo, Shi Ying, Sun Peng, and Wang Zhifang

Turenscape artists/sculptors: Qiu Qingyuan, Yie Zhijian, and Yie Jun.

Client: Zhongshan City

4.2 The People's Place: Dujiangyan Square

Commended Award, ar+d Emerging Architecture Awards, 2004

Kongjian Yu

The Graduate School of Landscape Architecture, Peking University and Turenscape, Beijing, China

Dujiangyan Square covers 11 hectares and is located in the middle of a dilapidated and featureless old townscape in Dujiangyan City. This city is a designated international tourism city near Chendu, Sichuan Province, China. In 1999, an international competition was held. Ten entries were selected for the short list and the final selected design was executed at the end of 2002.

This design was inspired by the unique regional natural and cultural landscapes, nearby irrigation works, and local traditions. With a budget of less than $US40 per square meter, the project is new urban space that tells ancient stories using a new design vocabulary. This modern design language expresses the regional and local identity in a new approach. The project was also designed to attract tourists as well as accommodate the daily needs of the local citizens.

1 Where: the Region and the Site

In a legendary basin surrounded by high mountains, Chengdu is agriculturally one of the most productive and romantic places, described in Chinese as the "land of heaven". It is also one of the most densely inhabited areas. The city Dujiangyan was historically named as the Irrigation County after the famous ancient irrigation works, the Dujianyan Weir. The prosperity of the area has been dependent on this historic infrastructure project. The weir, a world cultural heritage site, was built more than 2000 years ago, and is still in use today.

The site was a former derelict urban area, and was cleared and eliminated before the design competition was held. It is located approximately 2 kilometers from the famous Dujiangyan Weir. The canal diverted from the weir is divided into three irrigation canals that run through this site.

2 Project Purpose

According to the competition brief, the submission must meet the following requirements:

1 To improve the landscape of the downtown area and provide a public, open space for local residents

2 To tell the cultural and historical stories of the city, especially the stories of irrigation works that gave the city its reputation

3 To become a tourist attraction.

3 Philosophy and Design Intentions

The design strategy was based on careful site analysis and understanding of the local and regional landscape. Listening to the residents' experiences also helped to understand daily life and create social context and sensitivity for the design approach. This approach helped the designers understand the spirit of the place.

4 Challenges and Solutions

Located in the center of a busy and featureless urban area, the project faced many challenges including:

1 Transportation: a main street across the existing site divides the square into south and north areas. To resolve this incongruous and physical barrier, the designers created an underpass with sunken water squares at each end as a form of spatial linkage.

2 Water accessibility: the slopes of the three irrigation canals are steep, with rapid water flows, and could not be modified due to water management regulations. The design made use of the elevation difference to divert water from the upper reach of the canals and create a creek in the square, allowing the water to become accessible.

3 Fragmentation and identity: rapid canals fragmented the square. A formal and symbolic language was developed using the bamboo basket as a reference. As a paving pattern, this bamboo basket in the horizontal plane acts as the unifying element. As the main field of pavement, it gives a form of identity and creates uniformity to this public space. The overall layout of the square resembles an unfolding bamboo basket that radiates from a focal point. A sculpture stands at

the focal point. The lighting columns, the carved stone walls, and fences also use the bamboo basket as a design reference.

5 Design Inspiration

In addition to formulating strategies that make the square functional, aesthetic issues and symbolism are utilized in the overall design approach. The designers took their design cues and inspirations from careful research as follows:

1 The folklore of Dujiangyan Weir: Li Bin, the inventor of the famous weir, tried various techniques to build the strongest weir against floods. He tossed treasure stones into the waves as tributes to the river goddess for advice. He was inspired to use gentle devices, such as bamboo baskets containing pebbles, against the strongest forces. Wooden poles constructed in triplets were also employed. For 2000 years, these simple weir-making techniques have been the most effective, economic, and durable methods, stronger than steel and concrete. This technique is still in use today. Fish mouths (triangle-shaped dividers) and flumes were also inspirations for the square's design vocabulary.

2 The regional landscape: the surrounding physical area includes agricultural landscapes and their associated field patterns. Areas of rapeseed blossoms also contribute to the region's physique. Local vernacular architecture utilizes wooden frame structures, and stone walls. These provide references for elements of the project's design.

3 Lifestyle: Dujiangyan City is well known for its leisurely lifestyle. This is a result of the influence of the nearby famous weir and historical transformation of the basin into a productive and worry-free "land of heaven". Socially, the city is active: people meet in groups, play cards in groups and like to sit in the sun. A strong work ethic and family values exist and are part of the project's design inspiration.

6 Important Features of the Design

1 The layout: in response to the site topography, the plan consists of a pattern radiating from a central sculptural focal point. A system of various water features was integrated into the overall design, utilizing the vertical shifts in elevation, and allowing the water features to be accessible for pedestrians. Numerous native camphor trees were planted to provide shade, and the fragmented pieces were formally unified with a visual language abstracted from the bamboo basket.

2 The central axis: the focal sculpture, a "piece of jade contributed to the river goddess", is on the main axis along with three lighting columns, a 100-meter-long carved stone wall, and a meandering creek. Water is diverted from the upper reach of the canal and flows in this meandering creek along the axis. This central axis is diagonal and visually connects the pedestrian street at the south end and the valley located kilometers away in the north, where the famous ancient weir is located. The focal sculpture is 30 meters high and 3 meters wide, and is made of granite. Water has been used in the design of the base. The carved stonewall is used to create spatial variety, strengthen the central axis, and represents the local vernacular architecture.

3 Artworks: some of the important artworks include the metal gold canopy, hung on tilted bronze poles that collectively assemble the wooden triplets used in the ancient irrigation works. The golden canopy also recalls the experience of the rapeseed blossom areas.

4 People spaces: various spaces are allocated in different parts of the square. These are designed with the local culture and social traditions including: 5-square-meter seating boxes designed for groups to play cards, noted as being the favorite local game. A sunken amphitheater, and three sunken water spaces, are designed for people to enjoy water features. The fountains are designed interactively for people to play. Seating is provided next to the canals.

This new public space is intended to provide a narrative landscape that represents local tradition, spirit of the place, local heritage, and the city's lifestyle.

Project Location: Dujianyan City/Sichuan, China

Size: 10.7 hectares

Date of Completion: December, 2002

Owner/Client: Government of Dujiang Yan City

Design Firm: Turenscape, Beijing, China

Design Principal: Kongjian Yu

Design Team: Kongjian Yu, Shi Ying, Lin Shihong, Guo Xuanchang

Photography: Yu, K.J. and Cao, Y.

Figure 13 Place for play: water surface features many fish mouths that emanate from the base of the sculpture. The waves created by the small fish mouths create a dynamic reflective water surface that was inspired by the irrigation works and the bamboo weaving techniques used in the local daily handcraft traditions.

14

Figure 14 The land, site and people: the project is located in a highly populated province in China and in one of most productive and unique vernacular landscapes .

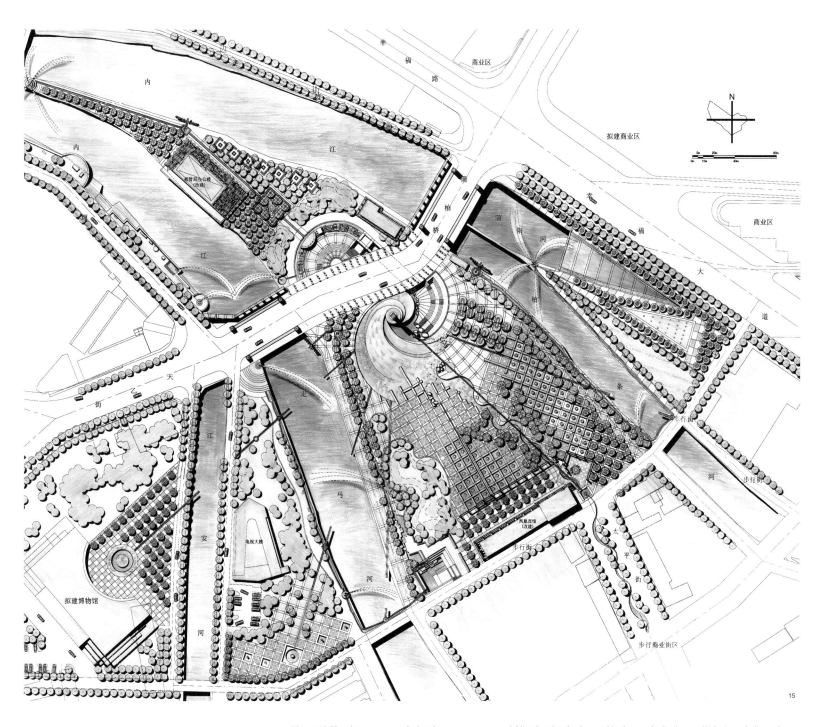

内
内
江
江
失
街
江
安
河

拟建博物馆

内

江

蒲
柏
桥

幸
福
路

商业区

拟建商业区

商业区

蒲
阳
河

幸
福
大
道

步行街

河

步行街

太
平
街

步行商业街区

地视大楼

马
河

凤凰宾馆
(改建)

步行街

15

Figure 15 The plan: pavement design that represents an unfolding bamboo basket used in the nearby Dujianyan Weir. A symbolic sculpture and water feature is located at the central focal point. A diagonal axis created by a carved stone wall juxtaposed with a meandering creek visually dominants the square. This axis connects the south part of the pedestrian street symbolically with the Dujianyan Weir located to the north.

171

rapeseed in blossoms

16

172

17a

Figures 16–17e Place for entertainment and exercise: Golden Canopy bronze poles inspired by the rapeseed blossoms and poles used in triplets at the irrigation works. It is one of many artworks in the square and is the location for various activities during different times. In the morning, women use the space for dancing and tai chi; at night tourists and residents come here to recall the experience of the bright and cheerful atmosphere created by the rapeseed blossoms in the warm spring. The Golden Canopy also provides shade for the musicians during festival time.

17b

17c

17d

17e

Figures 18, 19a,b Places for play: water surface features many fish mouths emanating from the base of the focal sculpture. The waves created by the small fish mouths create a dynamic water surface that reflects light. This was inspired by the irrigation works and the bamboo weaving techniques used in the local daily handcraft traditions.

19b

Figures 20a–e Making water accessible and playful: the slopes of the four irrigation canals are steep, with rapid water flows, and cannot be modified due to water management regulations. The design made use of the elevation differences to divert water from the upper reach of the canals in a traditional way. Red stones found in the local river are utilized in the design, allowing the water to become accessible, touchable, and playful.

21a

21b

21c

21d

Figures 21a–d The focal sculpture in a mist fountain: the iconic sculpture and lighting columns along the central axis recall the unique bamboo baskets used for building the Dujiangyan Weir. The columns are carved in granite, and illuminated from the interior. The ground represents a riverbed covered with a thin layer of water and pebbles of various sizes.

22a

22b

22c

Figures 22a–c Places for groups: 5-square-meter seating boxes are designed for groups of retired people to play cards and to socialize. Seats are located in the shade for leisure activities and protection.

4.2a Dujiangyan Square: Articulating A Narrative Public Open Space

Homage to the nearby 2400 year-old Dujiangyan Irrigation works

Mary G. Padua

University of Hong Kong Faculty of Architecture

Turenscape tells an ancient story through the medium of a designed landscape. A narrative structure is created and is inspired by the nearby world heritage site, the Dujiangyan Irrigation Works. The story is also inspired by the local culture that helped to create this ancient infrastructure project.

As an invited critic for the project, I am curious about the place. Where is this project located? What is the local and regional context? What previously existed on the site? I am also curious about the temporal aspects of the project. How will the project change over time?

To structure a review of Dujiangyan Square, this essay has been organized to include: a brief cultural and historical background of the site and area context, a discussion of narrative and metaphor, project review and analysis, the use of water as a design element in contemporary landscape architecture, the designer's intentions, and a discussion of the project within the framework of place-making and urban regeneration.

Cultural and Historical Context

The area's historical and cultural context drives Turenscape's inspiration for the project design. Dujiangyan, formerly known as Guanxian, is located 60 kilometers northwest of Chengdu, the provincial capital of Sichuan. Sichuan province has been established as culturally significant and was a major cradle of Chinese civilization during ancient times. It is also known as "heavenly kingdom" due to its rich agricultural resources that are a result of the ancient irrigation works. This rich history provides a strong foundation for modern Sichuan's identity, and the city of Dujiangyan.

From a historical perspective, land reform led to major public works that allowed the transformation of dry land into productive agricultural areas to thrive and feed armies. This occurred during the Qin period and was part of a larger strategy to unite ancient China. Dujiangyan in ancient Chinese translates as "Capital River Dam". It was a colossal, carefully planned public works project in the eastern half of the Eurasian continent, the first known in the middle third century BC.[1]

This engineering project was established to harness the Min River, one of the Yangtze River tributaries. The project was built under the provincial military governor, Li Bing, and was a multi-faceted infrastructure project with both military and economic claims. It was intended to alleviate a chronic flood danger, provide a new inland waterway for commercial and naval boat traffic, and more importantly irrigate agricultural fields over a vast area. Building this major infrastructure project involved the use of river rocks contained in bamboo baskets, and an artificial island made of piled stone to create a functional feature known as the "fish bite".

This technological wonder along with the Min River provided major sources of food to the area. The river became the community focus and brought with it the life and culture of the ancient Chinese local population. Ancient animist Shu religion regarded the Min River as a deity. Various ancient local customs and beliefs were formed around the sacred aspects of the Min River and created folklore that is still believed today.

The Dujiangyan Irrigation Works continues to operate and function today. Its significance as a major infrastructure project was recognized as a cultural contribution worldwide and was designated a world heritage site in 2000 by UNESCO. It is currently the site of various local and regional festivals. This ancient infrastructure project, its folklore and mythology, and various traditions provide the inspiration for Turenscape's design of a new public plaza as a major focal point and destination for the city of Dujiangyan.

The Narrative and Metaphor

It is critically important to understand that landscape is two things at once: a collection of material objects within a scene, and the ideas that make those objects meaningful.[2] The two are brought together in the act of interpretation and are therefore mutually constituted. In the case of the "designed landscape", we can easily formulate the same statement and make clear connections about a landscape that is meaningful and created by a designer—in this case the landscape architect. As many have pointed out, landscape is both site and sight—both "what is seen" and a "way of seeing". Landscape interpretation requires a deliberate act of looking by a certain distancing for the spaces of everyday life. So it is also critically important to distinguish "landscape" from "place". Places are experiences; landscapes are interpreted.

Landscape is everywhere and we can learn important lessons by interpreting what we see in a methodical manner. Landscape interpretation is contextual (linked to a specific site) and situational (it asks: who is interpreting and why).[3] In the case of the designed landscape, Dujiangyan Square, Turenscape has made specific interpretations of the cultural aspects of the geographical area, using metaphors for design, and "borrowing" from the memories of the area. Spiro Kostof reminds us that architecture is inextricably bound in both "settings" and "rituals".[4] Similarly, the designed landscape also falls within these boundaries.

Peirce Lewis' seminal work, *Axioms for Reading the Landscape,* and his notions about cultural landscape, apply in Turenscape's efforts to read and interpret the landscape of this region. Peirce Lewis' axioms, while worth noting, should be read within the context of the essay for which it was written.[5] As such:

1 Landscape as clue to culture
2 Cultural unity and landscape equality
3 Common things
4 History
5 Geography/ecology
6 Environmental control
7 Landscape obscurity

"Landscape reading" has grown as a basis for teaching this method and notions of cultural landscapes. While this method is about cultural landscapes, some critics now believe that designed landscapes may meet the test for Lewis' axioms. For further thoughts on the local vernacular, other valuable lessons could be learned from essays written in J.B. Jackson's *Discovering the Vernacular Landscape*.[6]

Turenscape's design of Dujiangyan Square was clearly inspired by the nearby ancient infrastructure project. Turenscape also borrows from the agricultural heritage of the region through its use of plant materials and as inspiration for the water features and sculptures. References to the bamboo basket are used to create a new design vocabulary for the project. The social and cultural fabric of the city itself is also incorporated into the design. Borrowed elements from several of these layers are incorporated into the overall design and contribute to this unique narrative landscape.

Analysis

Dujiangyan Square replaces an old park in a derelict area of Dujiangyan. It covers 11 hectares and local municipal officials' objectives were to regenerate this part of the city. Other local government requirements called for:

• the improvement of downtown's landscape

• the provision of public open space for the local residents

• the creation of a link to the nearby World Heritage site, the Dujiangyan irrigation work

• the creation of a tourist attraction and destination.

Turenscape was selected through an international design competition process held in 1999. Its design approach was based on the genus loci where its philosophy of landscape architecture is based on deriving design clues from the site, the area, and other various factors. In particular, Turenscape saw its charge to find and capture the essence of the place and provide a narrative through the medium of landscape architecture— a contemporary landscape that portrays the history of the nearby Dujiangyan Irrigation Works, the region, its people, and folklore.

Physically, the project was constrained by many elements:

• a major vehicular corridor that crosses and separates the site

• the structure and location of the water canals were fixed and unchangeable

• a fragmented and derelict site.

Turenscape viewed these constraining elements as design opportunities, and explored ways that would help weave the site together, to create a new identity and "sense of place". This new public square was designed to meet the requirements of the local municipal authorities.

Turenscape tackled the challenge of the site's discontinuity created by the road by submerging it and building an underpass that would unite the main northern and southern parts of the project. To create access water to the water's edge, Turenscape utilized the vertical elevation differences of the adjacent canals and introduced a creek into the plaza design. To mitigate against the segregating character of the canals, Turenscape devised a design strategy that imposed a new formal and symbolic language in the form of sculpture and horizontal elements.

Turenscape utilizes an ordered and structured geometry that is based on a "center" or focal point. In this case, the center is a 30-meter-high water tower carved in stone, and its design is meant to evoke the local folklore and mythology of the Min River as goddess, and provide a visual landmark for the area. At the same time, Turenscape invokes a geometric paving design that symbolizes an unfolding bamboo basket. This design vocabulary references the bamboo baskets and rocks that were used to build the nearby ancient Dujiangyan irrigation works. Emanating from the central water tower is a series of three shorter towers and carved linear stonewall (aqueduct) that extends across the plaza to the boundary of the site. Along this dominating rectilinear element, and spouting from the base of the central focal point, Turenscape introduces a curvilinear creek where park visitors are allowed to interact with the water.

Turenscape was able to create a new landscape form for the area. Five discrete precincts are distinguishable in this large-scale public plaza as various "outdoor rooms" or sub-areas. The variety of spaces and the sounds from the raging water are a reminder of the moving water that envelops the site. The use of water throughout the site is the most distinctive design feature and dominating aspect of the site. The project is reminiscent of the work of Lawrence Halprin (1916–), a living legend and landscape architect from California. Turenscape's gestures echo ways Halprin uses water in projects such as Freeway Park, Seattle, Washington; Lovejoy Fountain, Portland, Oregon, and Levi Strauss Plaza, San Francisco, California.[7]

As a means of experiencing the project, the following precincts have been identified:

1 Prelude/agricultural field
2 Camphor orchard
3 Water celebration
4 Stage
5 Contrast of green and blue

Prelude/agricultural field

As one of the major gateways and urban entry points to the plaza, the "prelude" or entry plaza sets the stage for the coming series of pedestrian events in this new open space. Like a musical score, this prelude acts as the introduction to the rest of the design composition of the plaza. This forecourt is a quiet inviting space that uses lawn in geometric forms that evoke a larger field of green landscape, reminiscent of the nearby agricultural fields. The tall stone tower at the center of the site remains a dominant and constant feature. The scale of this area is small to medium and provides a starting point for experiencing Dujiangyan Square.

Camphor orchard

This has been called the camphor orchard because of the ordered way the trees are laid out. It is reminiscent of the physical form of agricultural orchards and the nearby agricultural farms. Within the camphor orchard is a variety of sitting areas, and places to view the canals. Along one side of the camphor orchard, the sculptural focal point of the site appears. The "edge" of this precinct is created by the linear stonewall that emanates from the 30-meter-high central water sculpture.

This stonewall is a screen that allows pedestrians to walk through from one area of the site to another, a design device that also creates a transition from one place to another. The style and design vocabulary of the stone screen wall borrows from the woven bamboo baskets used to build the nearby ancient dam. Along the more urban edge of the camphor orchard is the urban fabric of the city. Also, along one edge is the sunken water plaza that is part of the central water feature.

Water celebration

The climax of the site is the dominant, centrally located water tower. It is a formal 30-meter-tall sculpture that appears to symbolically celebrate water, and perhaps, abstractly, harkens back to the ancient irrigation works nearby. The red stones in the water pond are reminiscent of the rocks found in the Min River. The paving design is a reference to the bamboo baskets used in the nearby ancient irrigation works. Will park users comprehend this symbolic gesture? Or is it enough for the user to ponder the significance of the various water elements and enjoy the experience of the place?

The success of the project is demonstrated by the various users of this new open space during different times of the day. The local population utilized the park, even during the overcast cool autumn October weather when I visited. In the evening, many park strollers would take photos in front of the central water tower.

The water from the tower is channeled into a creek-like form that weaves under the linear stone screen wall. Trees and plants align edges of the creek creating a different experience from the central focal point and the hardscape around it.

South of the focal point is a grid of water fountains that perform different functions, such as bubbling and misting. It provides a surreal backdrop to the early morning tai chi practitioners. Ultimately, this area will be more successful as a foreground plaza to future building along this edge of the site. Equally, the sunken water garden will have more design meaning once a new building is in place.

Stage

The stage or amphitheater northwest of the "water celebration" provides another focal point for a place where people can gather and watch performances, either planned or impromptu. The smaller seating squares in this sub-precinct provide places for groups of people to play games and picnic, a local pastime. As one moves further along, there is an interesting small-scale intimate space with trees and large boulders that are reminiscent of the ancient irrigation works. This place is most intriguing, as one can hear the sounds of the adjacent water, see the raging water, and imagine the river where these large boulders came from. The mature trees provide sufficient cover to create the sense of intimacy that some places in nature might give.

Contrast of green and blue

The precinct of "contrasting green and blue" is a metaphor and creates a contrast between agriculture and urbanism. The large field of green lawn contrasts with the adjacent water. When viewed as a symbolic gesture of agriculture, it is in contrast with the adjacent hard paved area that contains a stage, and Turenscape's Golden Canopy, a much more urban part of the project.

This area is highly used as an impromptu performance area for tai chi and other forms of entertainment. As a gesture toward integrating and weaving the park into the urban fabric, this area succeeds.

Within each of the precincts described, a variety of places have been created. Ample areas for walking and gathering are provided. Water elements are used in various ways and the project offers locations that are human in scale. A hierarchy of landscaped and hardscaped areas are distributed throughout the project systematically. These are integrated by a series of water features: hard-edged channels, curvilinear creek, and a variety of water fountains. The sound of the adjacent raging waters provides an interesting acoustical context in various areas of the site, and Turenscape was able to maximize this sensual aspect in their sensitivity to design. While the overall project is grand in its scale, it pays homage to the nearby ancient irrigation works. The materials that are used are durable and long lasting. The place is being used by the local population. As a project to regenerate downtown Dujiangyan, the project's use along with the passage of time will provide evidence for its success.

Water Use in Landscape Architecture

To provide a larger global design context, it is critical to point out the way water as a design element has been used historically, and in contemporary landscape architecture. In the western renaissance, Italians were the masters of using water as a spectacle. The ultimate example is the Villa d'Este, where water was used to create a musical water organ, and channeled to create

various forms of ordered water fountains in different forms, such as spraying and arching. In the scholar gardens of the Jiangnan style, water is used as a backdrop, and is always still, never in motion. In the historic Moghul gardens located in the veil of Kashmir, water is used as a transportation mode, and is part of a religious procession. A series of movements and events occur in the Moghul garden: arrival pavilions, eating, and sleeping pavilions. In the 19th-century park-building movement in Western Europe and the United States, water is represented as lakes or ponds in pastoral-like landscapes.

By the 1960s, public spaces were being designed as part of the urban fabric.

These public spaces became the canvas for Lawrence Halprin, a world-renowned Californian landscape architect, who has been awarded numerous medals and awards throughout his career. His career was built on the celebration of water inspired by nature. The parks and public places he built were inspired by the water's source and its relationship to nature. Seminal works included Lovejoy Plaza, Seattle Freeway Park, and Franklin D. Roosevelt Plaza. He was probably the first to reintroduce water as a theme in the public realm in the United States. Corporate landscape architects, such as SWA, EDAW, and others followed suit in their use of water elements in both public spaces and private corporate landscapes.

In response to the environmental movement of the 1960s and 1970s, water became ecologically charged, and later landscape architects became more involved in the design of water treatment plants and wetlands design. By the late 1980s and

1990s, landscape architects returned to ideas of landscape architecture as a fine art, using water as a design element, not in ecological terms. A few landscape architects attempt to weave art and science in their expression of the use of water. George Hargreaves and his attempts to design the Guadalupe River Park corridor is an example of this. Betsy Damon and Margie Ruddick demonstrate how to clean water in the Living Water Garden in nearby Chengdu, allegedly the first of its kind. Although, often the idea of cleaning polluted water is often discussed in design studios in many western universities.[9]

Place-making and Urban Regeneration

Turenscape's use of water as a landscape design element is part of an emerging profession of landscape architecture in China. Water is active in Turenscape's garden, whereas generally in the classic Chinese scholar garden, water is passive. While water is the dominant theme, it is inspired by an ancient public works project, and the heritage and folklore surrounding its creation. Lawrence Halprin took his design cues for fountain design from the nearby Sierra Nevada mountain range in California. The design expression of Halprin's water-dominated parks and plazas were intended as focal points; his urban parks and plazas were responsive to the adjacent urban fabric and did not imbue any overlay of cultural heritage, whereas clearly Turenscape's design approach embraces the local cultural context.

Dujiangyan Square's design is strengthened by the culture and sensitivity to regional "place" and vernacular landscape. The raging torrential water in the adjacent canals bounds the site and its surrounding sound weaves the site together. The introduction of water elements and all of the forms that Turenscape introduces fields of misting fountains, a central sculptural water fountain, creek, and sunken water gardens are all orchestrated as part of a larger new celebration of the ancient Dujiangyan irrigation project.

Turenscape's narrative structure of the area's cultural heritage and use of water gives Dujiangyan Square a revitalized identity. This new place offers a unique backdrop for the cityscape and enhances the city's identity. Its strategic location offers this area of the city the potential for urban regeneration and its ongoing efforts as an international tourist destination.

Endnotes

1. *See Chapter 5, Ancient Sichuan and the Unification of China, by Steven F. Sage for a comprehensive discussion of the Duijiangyan inception and relationship to land reform, endeavors in war and agriculture.*

2. *See Cosgrove 1985; Mitchell 1996; Corner 1999*

3. *See Meyer, 1997*

4. *See Kostof, 1985*

5. *See Lewis*

6. *See Jackson, 1984*

7. *See Chronology in Lawrence Halprin: Changing Places*

8. *See Thompson*

9. *Based on author's conversations with studio teachers, Margie Ruddick (Harvard, U. of Pennsylvania), Pamela Burton (Sci-Arc, USC), Margaret Crawford (Harvard), John Kaliski (Sci-Arch, U. of Michigan)*

References

Baker, Alan R.H. 1992. Introduction: On Ideology and Landscape. In Alan R. H. Baker and Gideon Biger, Eds, Ideology and landscape in Historical Perspective. Cambridge: Cambridge University Press.

Corner, James (ed.) 1999. Recovering Landscape: Essays in Contemporary Landscape Architecture. Princeton Architectural Press.

Cosgrove, Denis 1985. Prospect, Perspective and the Evolution of the Landscape Idea. Transactions of the Institute of British Geographers. 10:45–67

Fried, Helene 1986. Lawrence Halprin: Changing Places. San Francisco Museum of Art, San Francisco, California.

Golley, Frank B. 1998. A Primer for Environmental Literacy. New Haven: Yale University Press.

Jackson, J.B. 1984 Discovering the Vernacular Landscape. New Haven:Yale University Press.

Kostof, Spiro, A History of Architecture: Settings and Rituals, New York: Oxford University Press.

Lewis, Peirce, 1979. Axioms for Reading the Landscape: Some Guides to the American Scene. In The Interpretation of Ordinary Landscapes, edited by Donald Meinig, Oxford: Oxford University Press.

Meyer, Elizabeth K. 1997. The Expanded Field of Landscape Architecture. In Ecological Design and Planning, edited by George F. Thompson and Frederick R. Steiner. New York: John Wiley and Sons.

Mitchell, W.J.T. (ed) 1994 Landscape and Power. Chicago: University of Chicago Press.

Thompson, J. William, The Poetics of Stormwater, Landscape Architecture, Vol 89, Number 1, Washington: American Society of Landscape Architects, 1996, 132–139, 144, 146.

About The Editors

Dr Kongjian Yu was awarded his Doctor of Design Degree at The Harvard Graduate School of Design in 1995. He is also the founder and dean of the Graduate School of Landscape Architecture at Peking University, and the founder and president of Turenscape, an internationally awarded firm with more than 200 professionals and one of the first and largest private landscape architecture firms in China.

Dr Yu has practiced actively and has been awarded four ASLA Honor Awards for planning and design, in 2002 and 2005, and 2006, by the American Society of Landscape Architecture. Dr Yu is also the winner of the National Gold Medal of Fine Arts (2004, the Cultural Ministry, China), and twice winner of the Human Habitat Model Award for designed projects (2002, 2005, the Construction Ministry, China). In 2004, he was awarded the Overseas Chinese Pioneer Achievement Medal by the Chinese central government for his overall contribution to the nation.

Dr Yu has published widely, including more than 150 papers and 15 books. His major research interests include the theory and method of landscape architecture and urban planning; the cultural aspect of landscape; landscape security patterns, and ecological infrastructure.

Mary G. Padua is Assistant Professor at the Architecture Department, Hong Kong University. She gained her BA in Landscape Architecture at UC Berkeley, an MA in Architecture and Urban Design at UCLA, and now is a PhD candidate at the Edinburgh College of the Arts, University of Edinburgh. She is the author of the book *Urban Funk* (Hong Kong, University Press, 2003), and several articles about contemporary landscape design in China.